RISK AND THE ENVIRONMENT

IMPROVING REGULATORY DECISION MAKING

D0826140

JUNE 1993

A Report of the

CARNEGIE COMMISSION
ON SCIENCE, TECHNOLOGY, AND GOVERNMENT

ISBN 1-881054-13-6

Printed in the United States of America

CONTENTS

FOREWORD

In the 23 years since Earth Day 1970, public concern has grown about government's ability to protect human health and the environment. Dioxin, Alar, food additives, second-hand smoke in the workplace (and elsewhere), lead, cellular telephones, and greenhouse gases are but a handful of the potential risk sources that have found a place in the public mind. Perceptions of danger—and attention spans—fluctuate as new science and new public relations efforts come to the fore. At the same time, concern about the cost of environmental and risk-related regulation has also risen.

Use of certain economic tools is probably the most concrete and persistent legacy of governmental attempts rationally to accommodate our desire for maximal safety at minimal cost. Cost–benefit analysis now permeates regulatory practice, and economic incentives focusing on total costs are gaining favor over "command and control" regulation. Indeed, the chief executive officer of a major chemical company recently called upon industry to take the bold step of incorporating the full social costs of chemicals into their market price.

Economic tools such as cost–benefit analysis are not magic bullets, however. Some regulatory benefits — protection of endangered species, for example — resist sensible quantification. How to evaluate the "costs" can also be problematic. Job losses caused by regulation in one segment of industry may be compensated for with creation of new jobs in another. For example, the sharp growth many observers expect in the nascent environmental technology industry as a result of increased regulation may outweigh any negative effects of regulation. Because of this unpredictability, superficial cost–benefit analyses may mislead decision makers.

Like economic analysis, the scientific basis for regulation is riddled with uncertainties, and like economic analysis, even at its best science fails to answer most of the hard questions in regulation. This report wisely acknowledges science's limitations in regulatory decision making, even as it reaffirms its importance. The report provides a menu of ideas for renovating the federal government's infrastructure for "environmental and risk-related regulation," or that regulation done by the Environmental Protection Agency (EPA), the Food and Drug Administration (FDA), the Occupational Safety and Health Administration (OSHA), and the Consumer Product Safety Commission (CPSC). Each of these ideas by itself could bring significant improvement if implemented. Taken as a whole, however, the ideas present a uniquely comprehensive and integrative institutional vision for regulation. We believe it is a vision of a more effective and efficient regulatory system.

Although the report addresses the full sweep of environmental and risk-related regulation, it frequently zeroes in first on the experiences of EPA, whose budget is by far the largest of the four environmental and risk-related agencies, using that agency as a case study from which conclusions can be generalized. Second in relative emphasis is FDA, an agency that existed for more than 60 years before the first of the others was created.

The report frankly criticizes certain past practices and arrangements, but displays no bias for or against stringent regulation. This is perhaps best exemplified in the report's unfavorable evaluation of regulatory review by the Executive Office of the President as conducted in recent years. The report recommends that case-by-case review be deemphasized in favor of broad forward-looking guidance by the Executive Office. Such a change would take account of the Executive Office's unique institutional position to examine issues that cut across all federal departments and agencies. It would increase efficiency, allowing a President to obtain greater environmental protection for the same cost as the old system, *or* less cost for the same amount of environmental protection.

We commend the Task Force's Chair, Helene L. Kaplan, the Chair of its Regulatory Subgroup, Douglas M. Costle, and the entire Task Force for the painstaking care they took over the past three years in producing this balanced, realistic, and very promising document. We urge the public and officials of all three branches of the federal government to consider it carefully.

William T. Golden, Co-Chair
Joshua Lederberg, Co-Chair

PREFACE

This report of the Carnegie Commission on Science, Technology, and Government was prepared by the Regulatory Subgroup of the Task Force on Science and Technology in Judicial and Regulatory Decision Making, in collaboration with the full Task Force. It was endorsed by the full Task Force at its meeting on October 16, 1992, and was approved by the Commission on November 30, 1992.

Members of the Task Force on Science and Technology in Judicial and Regulatory Decision Making were

Helene L. Kaplan
Chair

Douglas M. Costle
Regulatory Subgroup Chair

Alvin L. Alm*
Richard E. Ayres*
Sheila L. Birnbaum
Stephen G. Breyer*
Harry L. Carrico
Theodore Cooper*
E. Donald Elliott*
Kenneth Feinberg
Robert W. Kastenmeier
Donald Kennedy*
Francis McGovern
Richard A. Merrill*

Richard Meserve
Gilbert S. Omenn*
Joseph G. Perpich*
Paul D. Rheingold
Maurice Rosenberg
Oscar M. Ruebhausen
Pamela Ann Rymer
Irving S. Shapiro*
William K. Slate, II
Patricia M. Wald*
Jack B. Weinstein

* Member of Regulatory Subgroup

The Task Force held its first meeting in November 1989. The Task Force's Regulatory Subgroup first met in March 1990. Staff to the Regulatory Subgroup were

Jonathan Bender   Mark Schaefer
   Program Associate   *Senior Staff Associate*
Christina E. Halvorson
   Program Assistant

Thereafter, the Task Force and the Subgroup met several times each year, and participated in numerous teleconferences. Deliberations were aided by a series of papers prepared by consultants and staff. The Task Force developed its recommendation on an Office of Environmental Quality (see pages 43–45) in collaboration with two other Commission task forces, those on Environment and Energy and on the Organization of Federal Environmental R&D Programs.

Throughout its work, the Task Force sought to enlist advice and information from experts outside its ranks. A cross-section of practitioners and scholars shared their thoughts with us in letters, telephone conversations, and meetings. After the 1992 presidential election, Task Force members met with several transition officials, some of whom have since joined the new Administration, to discuss the Task Force's recommendations.

The Task Force will sponsor a number of activities to follow up its examination of regulatory decision making. Among these is a pilot project in which top officials from all three branches of the federal government will gather for an informal colloquy on risk management.

We note, finally, that events have to a degree overtaken the release of our report. At the time of this writing, the Clinton Administration has elected to eliminate the Council on Environmental Quality, in favor of an Office of Environmental Policy headed by a Deputy Assistant to the President. Moreover, press accounts[1] suggest that the Administration intends to implement significant reforms in the Office of Management and Budget's regulatory review program. Although the Office of Environmental Policy falls short of the level and strength that we recommend, both of these changes appear otherwise to be consistent with recommendations made in Chapter 2 of this report, and we are pleased that the new Administration has given early attention to the role of the Executive Office in regulation.

ACKNOWLEDGMENTS

We thank David Beckler and Stephen Gallagher, staff to the Task Force, for their contributions to our work. The Subgroup is grateful to Richard N. L. Andrews, Adam Finkel, Sheila Jasanoff, John Moore, Thomas O. McGarity, Charles W. Powers, Sidney Shapiro, Bruce L. R. Smith, and Arthur Upton for their thoughtful advice as consultants to the Subgroup and the Task Force. We thank Joan Z. Bernstein, David Doniger, Peter Hutt, Richard Stewart, and Michael Taylor for participating in a dialogue on the rulemaking process. We are grateful to Robert Barnard, Donald G. Barnes, Harvey Brooks, Gary Bryner, Douglas Ginsburg, Fred Hoerger, Christopher Kirtz, Franklin Mirer, Alan Morrison, Richard Pierce, Peter Strauss, Myron F. Uman, James D. Wilson, and Frank Young for providing the Subgroup with valuable information and advice. Finally, we wish to thank Bonnie P. Bisol for assisting in the release of the report, A. Bryce Hoflund and Simone Mechaly for assisting in production of the report, and Jesse H. Ausubel and David Z. Robinson for providing suggestions throughout the study.

As this report went to press, the Task Force learned the sad news of the death of their colleague Theodore Cooper. Dr. Cooper was an active and thoughtful contributor to this report; his counsel and encouragement were greatly appreciated.

EXECUTIVE SUMMARY

THE NEED FOR INNOVATION

The nation's environmental and risk-related regulatory agenda* has changed dramatically over the past twenty years, and it will undoubtedly continue to evolve in the decades ahead. Since the establishment of the Environmental Protection Agency (EPA), the Occupational Safety and Health Administration (OSHA), and the Consumer Product Safety Commission (CPSC) in the early 1970s, the cost and complexity of federal programs have increased as environmental and risk-related problems have become less amenable to straightforward solutions. In response to public demands for cleaner environments, healthier workplaces, and safer food and commercial products,

* We define "environmental and risk-related" regulation as regulation conducted by CPSC, EPA, FDA, and OSHA. The basis for the Task Force's decision to examine the environmental and risk-related subset of regulation, and to focus in particular on EPA and FDA, is discussed on pages 30–33.

policymakers are striving to develop innovative solutions to increasingly subtle and intractable problems.

We stand at a crossroads in environmental and risk-related regulatory policy, facing critical organizational and procedural questions about the future at a time of large budget deficits and escalating demands on the regulatory system. In order to address the challenges of the present and to anticipate and ameliorate the problems of the future, the nation must develop a more comprehensive and integrative decision-making infrastructure while maintaining the flexibility to adapt to the new challenges of the next century. Our report focuses on the interactions of science, technology, organizational dynamics, and law in environmental and risk-related regulatory policy and attempts to identify potential reforms. (See pages 35–36 for a "roadmap" to the report.)

FINDINGS AND RECOMMENDATIONS

EXECUTIVE OFFICE OF THE PRESIDENT: POLICY FORMULATION AND REGULATORY REVIEW

■ **The Executive Office of the President should expand its capacity to formulate broad environmental and risk-related policies and should better integrate these policies with other national goals** (see pages 43–48).

Federal policies to address environmental, health, and safety hazards are often inconsistent and fragmented. The need to develop comprehensive environmental and risk-related regulatory programs and to integrate them with the nation's economic, energy, and national security goals is paramount.

As the only entity in the federal government with a view of the whole regulatory landscape, the Executive Office of the President (EOP) is a logical focus for regulatory reform efforts. In recent years, unnecessarily high tension has existed between White House staff and agency regulators. The EOP has been accused of trying to "micromanage" technical details of rules that experts in regulatory agencies have prepared. Since the early 1970s, environmental and risk-related policymaking in the Executive Office has been largely reactive and at times, some have charged, obstructive. Policy activities in the White House have mainly focused on the economic impacts of regulatory actions, and the Executive Office has developed relatively few forward-looking initiatives to control threats to public health and the environment.

The Executive Office must have the capacity to undertake several fundamental tasks in the environmental, health, and safety policy arena (see Box 4, page 42). Of paramount importance is the capacity to identify and analyze issues of "presidential" significance; to develop integrated policies consistent with statutory mandates; to communicate these policies to responsible agencies, states, the public, and industry; and to monitor policy implementation.

In developing environmental and risk-reduction policies, the Executive Office should rely on the analytical capabilities of departments and agencies whenever possible. It should help the President to define the broad contours of the Administration's environmental and risk-related policy, but must take care to leave implementation details and day-to-day regulatory decisions to the regulatory agencies.

■ *A focal point should be created in the Executive Office of the President for developing environmental and risk-related policy in the context of other national policy goals (particularly economic) and for helping federal departments and agencies to integrate sustainable development and risk reduction objectives into their activities. By strengthening the existing Office of Environmental Quality (OEQ) and redefining its mission, this can be achieved without new legislation* (see pages 43–45). (On February 8, 1993, the White House announced its intention to abolish CEQ, and to replace it with an "Office of Environmental Policy." The new Office is to be staffed at approximately one-third the level of CEQ. It will be headed by a Deputy Assistant to the President.)

■ *The Executive Office's analytical and policymaking processes should complement and not supersede the capabilities in departments and agencies* (see pages 45–46).

■ *Cabinet-level working groups should be established to formulate and oversee the implementation of federal policies for environmental protection and risk reduction that cut across departmental boundaries. Standing groups should be created to address persistent concerns, such as the relationships among energy, environment, and the economy. Ad hoc groups should be created to address challenges that can be resolved over a limited period of time.* (see pages 46–47).

■ *The Office of Science and Technology Policy (OSTP) should play a leading role in developing environmental and risk-related policies by becoming more directly involved in policy decisions involving scientific and regulatory issues, promoting consistency in the scientific aspects of risk-based decisions, and ensuring that federal R&D programs are directed to the missions of the environmental and risk-related agencies. OSTP's work in these areas should be conducted in close cooperation with the Office of Environmental Quality* (see pages 47–48).

■ **Executive Office review of regulatory decisions made by the presidentially appointed administrators of federal agencies should consist primarily of an examination of the extent to which decisions are consistent with statutory mandates and broad Administration policies** (see pages 51–52).

Within broad statutory constraints, the approach a President takes to governing is largely a personal choice. Therefore, we do not recommend a precise mechanism for overseeing the activities of federal regulatory agencies. Nonetheless, general principles of good government should guide the executive review process in whatever form it takes (see pages 51–52).

The President should select appointees with whom a relationship of mutual trust can be established, and the President should be able to rely on the judgment of these appointees in implementing policies. If dissatisfied with the actions or progress of federal agencies, the President should either work with Congress to modify their legislative mandates or make changes in agency management. The Executive Office should not second-guess agency interpretations of statutes. It should appraise its capabilities realistically and should not review complex scientific or technical issues where it lacks the necessary expertise.

The Executive Office should have a minimum of regulatory review points, and the review process should be clearly described. Except for communication directly related to presidential deliberation, the executive oversight process should be open to public scrutiny. Economic analyses should take place chiefly at the agency level in the context of clearly stated procedural guidelines developed by the Executive Office.

CONGRESSIONAL, EXECUTIVE, AND JUDICIAL INTERACTIONS

■ **Mechanisms should be devised to promote informal communication among the branches of government with respect to environmental and risk-related issues** (see pages 59–63).

Congressional–Executive gridlock and other interbranch conflicts have impeded effective policymaking at times in the past. Although politically divided government has often contributed to this friction, interactions between Congress, the Executive, and the Judiciary can be contentious regardless of partisan differences. Increased informal communication among the branches could help alleviate some of this conflict. We propose two models designed to increase communication and foster better understanding among the branches.

■ *A forum should be created in which Members of Congress, executive branch officials, and judges can meet informally to discuss broad issues raised by the interaction of science and policy in environmental and risk-related regulation* (see pages 61–62).

■ *Informal working groups at both the principal and staff levels should be organized more frequently to foster communication between the executive and legislative branches in developing and implementing environmental policy* (see pages 62–63).

INTERAGENCY COORDINATION

■ **Mechanisms are needed to improve consistency in federal regulatory decision making and to facilitate interagency cooperation. One approach to meeting these needs is to establish a Regulatory Coordinating Committee comprised of the administrators of the environmental and risk-related regulatory agencies and representatives of the Executive Office of the President** (see pages 71–72).

The environmental and risk-related regulatory agencies have mandates that overlap in some areas and leave gaps in others. To ensure that agencies do not duplicate their efforts to reduce some risks while not attending to other hazards, a Regulatory Coordinating Committee should identify problems that necessitate or would benefit from the involvement of multiple agencies. Agency staff members should seek to build consensus on means for coordinating their efforts, and agency heads should review coordination issues that staff members cannot resolve. The committee should

■ Examine the relative risks posed by problems or categories of substances and attempt to identify problems that need additional attention; ensure that major risks that cross agency jurisdictions are addressed and that sufficient data are developed to rank them appropriately; and see that relative risk rankings are updated regularly as more information becomes available (relative risk analysis is discussed in more detail in the next section).

■ Develop and articulate a coordinated federal response to high-priority cross-cutting problems and set common risk reduction goals and strategies across agencies for these problems.

■ Develop methodologies and guidelines for risk assessment and risk management and promote the exchange of information among regulatory agencies. In areas where fully consistent approaches are found not to be appropriate, committee publications should explain why this is so and clearly describe the different approaches used by each agency. All committee publications should be readily available.

■ Identify research needs and determine the proper roles of individual agencies in meeting those needs, with agencies utilizing the research strengths of other agencies to the extent possible.

Science, Risk, and Regulatory Decision Making

■ **Agencies should place problems in broad risk categories and develop strategies to address risks of high priority. To do this, each regulatory agency addressing environmental and risk-related issues should develop a broad-based risk inventory. The agencies should use the inventories' output to help develop multidimensional risk rankings. The agencies should experiment with methods to integrate societal values into relative risk analyses where statutes do not supply all the value judgments necessary to rank risks. Agencies should repeat relative risk analysis initiatives periodically, readjusting the process at each iteration in light of lessons learned, new information, and progress in addressing high-priority risks** (see pages 75–90).

Setting priorities is the fundamental problem in regulatory decision making at the agency level, as at the presidential and interagency level. Comparing and ranking individual risks, families of risks, and risk reduction opportunities present great challenges for science-based regulatory agencies. The public, the media, industry, the Executive Office of the President, legislators, and the courts all exert pressure on these agencies, and their decisions often appear equal to the vector sum of these forces. While our regulatory agencies should be responsive to government institutions and the public, setting priorities on a "chemical of the month" basis may result in overregulation of some hazards, underregulation of others, and decreased agency credibility.

We see relative risk analysis as a promising way to promote scientifically sound decision making about risk. Nevertheless, we recognize that the technique is still in its infancy. To enhance the accuracy and credibility of the process, two components of relative risk analysis must be strengthened: scientific data must be better collected, organized, and evaluated, and more attention must be devoted to integrating societal values into the process.

■ *We recommend that other agencies working to reduce risk conduct relative risk analyses of the type done by EPA in* Unfinished Business *and* Reducing Risks *and that both EPA and these agencies periodically update their findings and methodologies* (see pages 81–82).

■ *We recommend that each agency develop a risk data inventory that reflects the agency's mission and that agencies coordinate their efforts to facilitate exchange of information and interagency comparability of risk rankings* (see pages 84–86).

■ Congress and regulatory agencies should consider modifying provisions and practices directed at protection of confidential business information in order to produce a better balance between industry's need for proprietary secrecy and the need for efficient use of environmental, health, and safety data by governmental agencies, the scientific community, and the public (see pages 86–87).

■ Regulatory agencies should report a range of risk estimates when assessing risk and communicating it to the public (see pages 87–88).

■ Agencies should experiment with different mechanisms for integrating societal values into the process of setting risk-based regulatory priorities (see pages 89–90).

■ Regulatory agencies should critically evaluate and take deliberate steps to improve their internal scientific capabilities and their means of integrating scientific and technological considerations into agency decision-making processes (see pages 90–94).

The Environmental Protection Agency recently convened a group of distinguished nongovernmental experts to examine its internal scientific capabilities and recommend approaches to improving the Office of Research and Development and its intramural laboratories. This analysis yielded many thoughtful recommendations. We believe that other agencies should undertake similar exercises.

■ Regulatory agencies should seek advice from other government agencies where appropriate expertise is available (see page 91).

■ Individuals with both public policy and scientific expertise should be appointed more frequently to senior positions in regulatory agencies (see pages 91–94).

■ The federal government should use its existing personnel authority to create opportunities for selected individuals to rotate in the early years of their careers through environmental and risk-related regulatory agencies, Congress, the Executive Office of the President, and, in some instances, administrative offices of the Judiciary (see pages 94–95).

Regulatory policy results from a dynamic interplay among politics, economics, law, ethics, and the physical and natural sciences. But relatively few scholars or practitioners of regulatory policy have a truly broad view. By providing new opportunities for promising staff members to rotate among the branches, the federal government will develop a highly trained and experienced cadre of individuals with a unique perspective that will eventually prove a valuable asset to the regulatory process. The protection accorded by the civil service system would help insulate these individuals from political influence.

LONG-RANGE GOALS AND STRATEGIES FOR REGULATORY PROGRAMS

■ **Regulatory agencies should establish specific long-term research and regulatory objectives and regularly report their progress toward achieving these goals to the President and Congress. Congress and the President should mandate that regulatory agencies justify annual budget and program plans in the context of explicit long-term regulatory goals. Furthermore, Congress should work more closely with federal and state regulatory officials and experts in nongovernmental organizations to devise realistic regulatory goals and deadlines for meeting them** (see pages 99–102).

Strategic planning is an essential but exceedingly difficult task for federal regulatory agencies. Congress and the agencies have traditionally been reactive rather than proactive in addressing environmental, health, and safety risks. We encourage Congress and the President to take a longer-range view in devising broad policy mandates and to give regulatory agencies more freedom to conduct internal strategic planning exercises.

In setting goals for federal agencies and mandating actions, Congress should match responsibilities with resources to ensure that objectives can be attained. Regulatory agencies should devise work plans and secondary goals to meet these long-term goals and should monitor progress in achieving them.

■ **Regulatory agencies should enhance their long-range planning capabilities by strengthening the linkages between research and regulatory policy-making efforts and by undertaking policy planning exercises in the context of relative risk analyses** (see pages 102–104).

The extent of linkages within regulatory agencies between research and development capabilities and the planning efforts of regulatory offices varies considerably. We believe that each regulatory agency should establish an anticipatory research program, closely linked with its regulatory program offices, to identify emerging problems and ways of addressing them.

■ *Regulatory agencies should strengthen their anticipatory research capabilities and establish and maintain effective linkages between these efforts and regulatory planning activities* (see page 103).

■ *Regulatory agencies should undertake long-term planning exercises in the context of the risk-based decision-making processes described in Chapter 5 of this report* (see pages 103–104).

■ *Regulatory agencies should sponsor extramural policy studies to expand and enhance agency intramural long-range planning processes* (see page 104).

RULEMAKING PROCEDURES

■ **Regulatory agencies should experiment actively with the variety of means available under existing authority to reduce rulemaking ossification. Care should be taken with all experiments to preserve adequate opportunities for analysis and public participation** (see pages 109–111).

The rulemaking process appears to have "ossified," becoming so time-consuming and expensive that agencies increasingly turn to perfunctory vehicles for promulgating policy, like policy statements, manuals, and regulatory letters. Any solution to the problems of "rulemaking ossification" must balance two sets of factors. Increased public participation and careful analysis of all aspects of a policy is desirable, but can lead to lengthy procedures—the very length and complexity of which may defeat the desirable ends of rulemaking itself. Although no "perfect" balance exists, providing a range of choices and criteria for making the proper choice would allow agencies to select the appropriate approach for each rule on a case-by-case basis.

The drafters of the Administrative Procedure Act intended it to provide agencies with a great deal of flexibility. Although judicial interpretations of the act have yielded a series of procedural requirements that somewhat constrain agency freedom, the zone of discretion remains wide. We present a set of suggestions for using this discretion to de-ossify the rulemaking process.

■ *Regulatory agencies should create a "menu" of procedures, ranging from highly simple to more complex, calling for various degrees of public participation and comment, which may be subject to varying degrees of judicial review, and whose legal status may also vary. Agencies could choose the kind of procedure they believe best fits the type of policy problem at hand from among the menu's options* (see page 110).

■ *Agencies should search for ways to diminish the complex, time-consuming nature of the informal rulemaking process* (see pages 110–111).

■ *Agencies should attempt to negotiate rules where it is possible to do so without prejudicing unrepresented third parties* (see page 111).

■ **Mechanisms should be explored to keep appropriate congressional committees informed of the interpretation made and ambiguities found by courts in the statutes that authorize rulemaking** (see pages 111–112).

Such efforts show promise in promoting clarity in the drafting of statutes. One approach is to have nonpartisan analysts periodically apprise relevant committees of statutes or statutory passages that have given rise to divergent interpretations. Another possible method is for committees with jurisdiction over regulatory statutes to devote one or two days per year to informal conferences with representatives of the agencies or the Executive Office of the President for this purpose.

■ **Executive Office officials should communicate less formally, earlier, and more directly with agency officials** (see page 112).

The current process—agencies submitting rules to the Executive Office, followed by EOP review for compliance with presidential policies—can create an adversarial relationship between the agencies and the White House, sometimes resulting in delay. Increased informal consultation and discussion earlier in the rulemaking process among staff members of agencies and the Executive Office would prove beneficial and would likely lead to faster approval of more effective regulations.

ROLE OF NONGOVERNMENTAL ORGANIZATIONS

■ **The extensive capabilities of nongovernmental organizations (NGOs) should be used more frequently to evaluate the regulatory process, suggest ways to improve existing regulatory strategies, and aid federal agencies in establishing regulatory priorities. Nongovernmental policy research organizations should establish stronger ties with scientists and engineers in universities to bolster their capacities to examine issues pertaining to environmental and health risks** (see pages 115–116).

Nongovernmental policy research centers can be particularly effective in convening a diverse group of practitioners and scholars for sustained reflection on problems of organization and decision making in environmental and risk-related regulation. The immense environmental challenges and health risks we face in the future, coupled with existing and anticipated constraints on the federal budget, will necessitate a considerable expansion of activity in the nongovernmental sector. Nongovernmental policy research organizations should establish stronger ties with scientists and engineers in universities to bolster their capacities to examine issues pertaining to environmental and health risks.

I

INTRODUCTION

One of the most important emerging roles of government in the past 20 years has been the regulation of escalating risks to human and ecological health arising from our ever-growing and ever more complex national and international economies. As awareness of global environmental problems such as global warming has added to existing anxiety about more local toxic threats (or potential threats), such as hazardous waste sites, the environment has moved to public policy's center stage. Closely allied are concerns about risks from toxic substances in still more local environments like the places in which we work, the consumer products we use, and the food we eat.

Ambitious legislative mandates and serious resource limitations, coupled with the divided government of the past decade, have combined to place extraordinary burdens on the federal regulatory apparatus we expect to safeguard us from, and teach us about, potential environmental risks. Still, U.S. regulatory programs are considered among the strongest in the world, and we can point to many accomplishments over the past two decades. For example, our system for assuring the safety of foods and drugs ranks among the best in the world, and our laws assuring a safe workplace are among the most comprehensive of any nation. And we have made significant progress in improving the quality of our air, land, and water resources.

Yet many goals remain unmet. Federal policies addressing environmental, health, and safety threats are often inconsistent and fragmented. There also is growing concern that our environmental regulatory programs may have placed too much emphasis on cancer-related risks (carcinogens in particular), and too little on non-cancer-related health risks, ecological risks, and the sustainable use of resources.[2]

The process of policymaking in this area warrants as much concern as the policies made. Many regulatory practices and arrangements appear ill-suited to coherent policy development and implementation. Priorities tend to be driven by crises rather than proactive deliberation. Regulatory agencies sometimes duplicate each other's efforts or, worse still, work at cross-purposes with each other. Conversely, some important problems do not fall squarely within existing agency jurisdictions and interests. Avoidable friction within and between the branches of the federal government dissipates resources desperately needed for more productive uses. To muddle through the quagmire a little more quickly, agencies often turn to methods for promulgating policy that provide for inadequate analysis and public participation. Expertise within and outside government is often poorly utilized.

To be sure, there have been improvements in the federal government's organization and decision-making processes for environmental, health, and safety regulation. Many of these are described in this report. But though much progress has been made, much remains to be accomplished. This report explores some of these decision-making processes and recommends a series of reforms in them. We believe that, if implemented, these recommendations will result in a more efficient, flexible, and forward-looking decision-making infrastructure, one better suited to meeting the challenges of the end of this century and the beginning of the next.

STRENGTHENED DECISION MAKING FOR A NEW AND CHANGING AGENDA

We focus in this report on regulatory activities of the Environmental Protection Agency (EPA), the Occupational Safety and Health Administration (OSHA), the Consumer Product Safety Commission (CPSC), and the Food and Drug Administration (FDA). Lacking a widely accepted term to describe this subset of the federal regulatory effort, we refer to it here as "environmental and risk-related" regulation.

A Crossroads in Policymaking

It appears to us that the nation has reached a crossroads in environmental and risk-related policymaking. Techniques to evaluate and control threats to human and ecological health have become more sophisticated as government has worked to answer the public's call for healthier workplaces, safer commercial products, and a cleaner environment. Yet the problems at times seem more intractable. Many of the most obvious opportunities for reducing risks from hazardous substances and problems have already been pursued. The risks that remain tend to be harder to characterize precisely and to reduce. And serious new problems that were unknown or that seemed peripheral ten or twenty years ago—global climate change, ozone depletion, biodiversity loss, and AIDS, to name but a few—have come to the fore. Experience suggests that the regulatory agenda will continue to change rapidly.

It is a time when new ideas are needed to push forward the frontiers of regulatory decision making. As William Ruckelshaus once noted, "The most interesting moments are those when the idea is on stage, when it engages the public in passionate debate, when people struggle to fit the idea into the existing order, and when, through their efforts, people inevitably change both the existing order and the character of the idea."[3] Fortunately, there is no shortage of good ideas for substantive change. Thoughtful suggestions for policy innovation stream constantly from the nongovernmental sector, industry, and all levels of government.

As society begins to move toward embracing the goal of sustainable development[4] in the wake of the 1992 United Nations Conference on Environment and Development in Rio de Janeiro, ideas are generated and refined even more quickly. An abundance of literature has been published in recent years on topics related to sustainability like economic incentives, low-waste/no-waste technology, water resource conservation, and habitat protection. Indeed, a diverse group of influential organizations have issued reports in just the last few months, some calling for dramatic change, on these topics.[5]

Our report is intended to complement, rather than supplement, such efforts. We have attempted to develop recommendations that will improve and streamline the federal decision-making *process*. We offer not policy advice, but ways in which the federal government can better sort through advice and information to develop and implement sound policy for the 1990s and beyond.

ISSUES DEFERRED

Our report covers a broad range of issues. Nonetheless, as is true of any report, much that is relevant could not be addressed. Two issues in particular bear mention.

First, many problems in environmental and risk-regulated regulation can be traced at least in part to flaws in substantive laws and in the legislative process itself. Some have recommended that to achieve sensible environmental regulation Congress should enact a single comprehensive act for EPA that would replace the patchwork of statutes it currently administers. More generally, considerable criticism has been directed at Congress's committee structure. Thorough examination of such matters would require several task forces. Our report, therefore, takes the current legal and legislative regime as a given and recommends a series of administrative reforms that will both optimize decision making within the current regime and be adaptable to new ones.

It should be noted that the matter of congressional organization is beginning to receive the attention it merits. The Carnegie Commission's Committee on Science, Technology, and Congress will release a report in the fall of 1993 on organizational and procedural reforms in Congress. The Center for Strategic and International Studies' Strengthening of America Commission, chaired by Senators Sam Nunn and Pete V. Domenici, recently issued a report addressing these issues, as has a joint Brookings Institution and American Enterprise Institute effort led by Thomas E. Mann and Norman J. Ornstein.[6] Moreover, the legislature's own recently created Joint Committee on the Organization of Congress will hold a series of hearings throughout 1993 and issue its recommendations by the end of the year.

Second, the states play a critical role in environmental and risk-related regulation. In policy areas where Congress has not preempted state regulation, the states often have their own regulatory regime to fill gaps in or to augment federal rules. Moreover, several federal statutes, perhaps most notably the Clean Air Act, require state governments to develop and administer detailed plans for implementing federally developed standards. As with substantive laws and the legislative process, however, a worthwhile examination of the state role in this area fell outside the scope of a report of this size. Another Carnegie Commission task force has addressed the broad issue of science and technology and the states,[7] but more in-depth inquiry into the state role in environmental and risk-related regulation is certainly warranted.

BROAD CONTEXT

To understand why we focus on this small subset of the vast enterprise of federal regulation, we must glance briefly at the full sweep of federal regulation. Although the report is primarily about noneconomic perspectives on regulation, it is useful to begin with a necessarily oversimplified description of the economic rationale for regulation.

ECONOMIC BASIS FOR REGULATION

Commerce in America is governed by markets, as a rule. In theory, when markets operate correctly they should account for hazards or other undesirable attributes of products with lower prices; hazards in jobs, conversely, should be reflected in higher wages. Society would "vote" with its pocketbook on the hazards it wishes to accept.

Government intervenes in markets where they do not operate properly. In the real world, a variety of malfunctions can, and frequently do, occur. For instance, the social cost of a product may not be reflected in the business costs (including lost profits) to the firm that produces it, creating what economists call an "externality." The classic example is air pollution. Where, as is often the case, the burden of air pollution falls largely on those who do not purchase the firm's product, the firm will not receive the correct signals from the market. Another example of a market failure is informational asymmetry. Consumers may have no way of knowing that a particular food additive is highly carcinogenic, or even that the food they eat contains the additive. As with an externality, when there is an informational asymmetry, the market does not propagate the message that consumers with knowledge would presumably send—"stop selling this product, because we will not buy it."[8]

ECONOMIC REGULATION VERSUS ENVIRONMENTAL, HEALTH, AND SAFETY REGULATION

Regulation is intended to correct market failures. Two basic categories of regulation exist, "economic regulation" and "environmental, health, and safety regulation." Federal regulation was initiated in the 19th century to deal with market imperfections whose symptoms were purely economic, such as monopoly.[9] With the creation of the Food and Drug Administration in 1906 the federal government began to regulate certain market failures that resulted in danger to public health from hazardous substances. Economic regulation ballooned in the 1930s and 1940s under President Roosevelt, largely as a response to the Depression. By contrast, regulation to protect environment, health, and safety, grew comparatively slowly during this period and for some decades thereafter. Agencies like the Federal Aviation Administration were organized to prevent catastrophic accidents from certain discrete activities. Relatively little additional attention was paid, however, to more diffuse and chronic threats, such as pollution, until 1970, when EPA was established. In the years immediately following, OSHA[10] was established to protect workers from on-the-job hazards, and CPSC was created to safeguard consumers from potentially harmful products.

Environmental and Risk-Related Regulation

Conceptually, the mission of the environmental and risk-related agencies, CPSC, EPA, FDA, and OSHA, overlap to a great extent. A large part of what each does is to protect the public from exposure to low levels of (nonnuclear) hazardous substances and problems. To carry out this mission, each of the agencies is vitally concerned with "risk" (see Box 1) and processes attendant to it: risk assessment, risk management, and risk communication (see Box 2). These agencies also draw on the same types of science and technology—often, in fact, they draw from the same science base and face a series of similar problems that lie at the interface of science, bureaucracy, politics, and law.

Significant precedent exists for considering these agencies and the work they do as a whole. The agencies were grouped together from 1977 to 1980 in the Interagency Regulatory Liaison Group, a coordination body (see pages 65–67). In 1983 the National Research Council published a seminal report on risk assessment (commonly known as "the Redbook") that also focused on these agencies, which it termed the "health and safety" agencies.[11]

Although the greatest commonality between the agencies is regulation of health risks posed by discrete substances, we decided against limiting our report to this domain alone. EPA and, to a lesser extent, the other agencies have always directed part of their regulatory activities at "problems" with multiple causes, rather than only at specific substances. Moreover, such problems extend beyond health. Government is paying increasing attention

---

Box 1. "Risk": A Multifaceted Term

The term "risk" is often given very different meanings at different times and by different speakers. We use "risk" in this report in two different senses. First, when discussing risk assessment of individual substances or problems, we intend risk to mean either the probability that an individual will suffer some adverse consequence as a result of exposure to a pollutant or pollutants or the consequences of such an exposure for an entire population (derived by multiplying the average of the individual probabilities by the number of individuals in question). This sense is normally used in the context of scientific risk assessment. It is the more straightforward use of the term, but even so there may be misunderstanding about what exactly a risk assessment of this kind means (see Boxes 7 and 8, pages 76–78).

The other sense in which we use risk can be described as a function of the probability of a harm occurring and the perceived *magnitude* of that harm. The subjectivity of the latter term frequently produces confusion and conflict. Different people tend to ascribe different magnitudes to the same consequence. For example, some individuals are concerned about a very small—perhaps one in a million—chance of developing cancer, while others might see this risk as trivial. It can be seen, in fact, that whether or not one calls the probability one in a million "very small" depends on how one evaluates the magnitude of the consequence at issue. The magnitude, in turn, is frequently determined by several components, and, again, different individuals will tend to value the components of the same harm differently. In evaluating the potential harm of smog, for instance, one person may consider only health effects, while another may also care about esthetic diminution. Moreover, a host of factors extrinsic to the evaluator influence the evaluation of the harm's magnitude, for instance whether or not exposure to the potential harm is voluntary. The use of risk in this sense is explored further in the "Value Integration" subsection of Chapter 5 (pages 88–90).

---

to repairing and preventing ecological degradation. Finally, many of the environmental challenges that government faces today—worldwide population growth for instance—transcend the conceptual boundaries of "risk." To take this larger, contemporary perspective into account, we chose the phrase "environmental and risk-related regulation" over simply "risk regulation," or the Redbook's "health and safety agencies."

We note that several other agencies are involved in one way or another with environmental and risk-related regulation, including the Department of Energy, the Department of Agriculture, and the Department of Housing and Urban Development. Many of this report's findings and recommendations will be germane to these agencies, even though they are not explicitly directed at them.

Box 2.   Definitions—Risk Assessment, Risk Management, Risk Communication

---

- **Risk assessment** is essentially the process of deciding how dangerous a substance is. The first step in the process of risk assessment is to identify and qualitatively describe the hazard to be assessed. Next, the level of exposure to the hazardous entity is estimated, along with the response of the organisms in question (usually humans, but sometimes, as when evaluating ecosystems, other species) to different dose levels, using the best scientific data available. Finally, the above information is combined to characterize the risk quantitatively. (See Box 7 on page 76 for more information on risk assessment).

- **Risk management** is the process of deciding what to do about an assessed risk or group of risks. Risk management, unlike risk assessment, explicitly involves consideration of a wide range of legal, economic, political, and sociological factors.

- **Risk communication** is the process by which agencies and individuals discuss risk with one another. Because perceptions of risks often differ widely, risk communication typically requires sensitivity and to the extent possible should involve genuine dialogue.

While it is often useful for analytical purposes to think of these functions as distinct processes, they frequently blend together in practice—see Box 8 on page 78.

THE CASE OF THE ENVIRONMENT

We frequently turn to EPA and environmental problems for case studies from which to develop more broadly applicable lessons. Next in comparative emphasis is FDA. In some instances we focus on EPA or FDA because one of them leads the other agencies in innovation or experience on one or another issue. EPA is funded at a much higher level than the other environmental and risk-related agencies, and FDA was born 64 years before the first of the others was created. At other times the report begins with one of these agencies as a point of departure simply for analytical convenience.

SPECIFIC CONTEXT

Three characteristics associated with the evolution of environmental and risk-related regulation stand out as critical: increased complexity, increased workload, and resource constraints, and the corresponding need for agencies to set priorities and anticipate problems before they become intractable.

Increased Complexity

Modern environmental and risk-related regulation can be said to date from the early 1970s, with the birth of EPA, OSHA, and CPSC. Responding to an upsurge of environmental concern and consumer advocacy among its constituents, Congress created these new agencies and has since enacted numerous laws for them to implement and enforce. The newly created responsibilities and redistribution of old duties colonized an institutional landscape on which FDA had stood alone.

Great new demands would eventually be placed on science. At first, however, dramatic progress could be made without testing science's ability to deliver. EPA's first Administrator, for instance, directed the agency's efforts at reducing emissions of gross pollutants that posed acknowledged risks to public health and the environment. Little technical insight was required to realize that preventing the passage of raw sewage into rivers would reduce disease and odor and increase fishability and swimmability. One did not have to understand chemistry to know that filtering the thick black smoke pouring out of a smokestack allowed persons living nearby to breathe easier and cough less.

Regulation, however, may involve diminishing returns. Progress is rapid at first, but each new incremental gain may be more difficult and more expensive to achieve. As noted earlier in this section, regulators have already taken many of the most accessible steps toward reducing risks from hazardous substances—yet significant residual risks remain. Today's environmental policymakers must also address problems with diffuse causes and effects that extend far in time and space, like stratospheric ozone depletion and global climate change. And a host of new technologies and technological applications, biotechnology perhaps notable among them, present new challenges for each of the agencies. Many of these problems and processes are only partially understood, and regulatory decisions must frequently be based on limited data and considerable scientific and technological uncertainty.

Increased Workload, Resource Constraints

Increased complexity has been accompanied by an expanding workload. In many instances, resources have not kept pace.

For example, between 1980 and 1985, EPA's staff decreased by approximately 10 percent,[12] even though the agency assumed responsibility for the substantial Comprehensive Environmental Response, Compensation, and Liability Act (CERCLA) in 1980; Congress also reauthorized and significantly expanded three other acts in EPA's jurisdiction during this period.[13]

At FDA the situation has been similar. For instance, imports of substances under the agency's jurisdiction tripled from 500,000 entries in 1971 to more than 1.5 million in 1990. Between 1985 and 1990, R&D expenditures in the pharmaceutical industry doubled, leading to a sharp upturn in applications for new products submitted to the FDA. In 1989, agency reviewers received 82 percent more applications than in 1980. From 1980 to 1988, FDA was required to implement 21 new laws and amendments, while its overall work force decreased by 11 percent.[14]

NEED TO SET PRIORITIES AND ANTICIPATE PROBLEMS

Expanding responsibilities and increasingly limited resources have compelled agency policymakers to make difficult choices about which risks to regulate first and what standards to set. The need for mechanisms to help policymakers set priorities has been increasingly felt. Risk assessment (see Boxes 7 and 8 on pages 76–78) has emerged as an increasingly common tool for this purpose. Risk assessments, though often crude and inexact, can be used both to provide a rough estimate of the danger posed by individual substances and to allow rough relative comparisons of risk levels among different hazards. Such procedures can help policymakers determine the severity of problems and provide guidance on where regulatory priorities should lie within a broad universe of diverse risks.

Studies such as EPA's landmark 1987 *Unfinished Business* report have shown that public perceptions of risk do not necessarily correspond with expert assessments.[15] As a result, much attention has focused on ways to improve communication between agency officials and the public in order to prioritize health and environmental hazards more appropriately.

In considering organizational frameworks and decision-making processes to develop and implement regulatory strategies, it is important to devise a dynamic policymaking system that can anticipate and respond to the challenges on the horizon as well as those confronting us today. A better capacity to identify emerging or potential problems will enable agencies to prevent environmental degradation and minimize public health threats before they become more difficult, and thus more expensive, to address. For example, the nation now faces a multibillion-dollar remediation effort to remove lead-based paint from homes and lead pipes and fittings from water systems.[16] Yet the toxicity of lead was recognized long before it became a common component of construction materials.[17] The problem we face today could have been minimized and serious health effects avoided, and hundreds of millions of dollars could have been saved, had the nation had a science-based regulatory system in place decades ago that could have anticipated this problem and taken steps to prevent it. As is often the case, the costs of past inaction far exceed the costs of prevention.

SCOPE OF THE REPORT

Many of our recommendations embody a preference for integrated rather than fragmented decision making and for agency-initiated cooperation rather than coordination mandated by the Executive Office of the President. Another recurring theme in many of these recommendations is that agency administrators and personnel should have primary responsibility for implementing statutory mandates. The Executive Office should provide broad guidance to top agency officials and then rely on these presidentially appointed and Senate-confirmed officials to make well-reasoned, legally sound decisions. At the same time, these agency officials must look beyond the traditional boundaries of their agencies in working to reduce risk. Environmental and health hazards seldom confine themselves to agency jurisdictions. Consequently, regulatory officials must work together to identify and minimize the most serious risks.

In the chapters that follow, we trace the institutions and mechanisms through which environmental and risk-related policy is established and implemented, following a "top-down" progression.

■ In Chapter 2, we examine the **role of the Executive Office of the President** in formulating and reviewing environmental and risk-related policy (see pages 37–53). We recommend that the Executive Office of the President (EOP) focus on developing broad policy directions and priorities for federal agencies. At the same time, it should avoid micromanaging agency decision making. The EOP should anticipate problems and identify opportunities for policy innovation instead of merely reacting to the actions of federal agencies.

■ In Chapter 3, we analyze **interactions among the three branches of government** in science-based regulation, arguing that more opportunities should be created and more use made of existing channels for informal interbranch communication in devising strategies to address environmental and health risks (see pages 54–63).

■ In Chapter 4, we explore **interagency coordination** and the challenges of devising integrated regulatory strategies (see pages 64–72). We argue that a new Regulatory Coordinating Committee comprised of the administrators of the various regulatory agencies and representatives of the Executive Office should be created to assure a coordinated and consistent response to high-priority problems.

■ In Chapter 5, we examine three intraagency functions found at the heart of regulatory decision making: **relative risk analysis, science advice, and personnel development** (see pages 73–95). We argue that policymakers should make greater use of relative risk analyses, while recognizing that risk-based decisions often involve a high degree of uncertainty. Risk analysis by nature involves value judgments, and agencies must experiment with means of reflecting the informed judgments of the citizenry in relative risk analyses.

■ In Chapter 6 we describe the importance of **long-range thinking** in regulatory agencies (see pages 96–104). We call for the agencies to devote more attention to articulating long-range goals and work to match resources with objectives. We also recommend that agencies develop specific milestones and report regularly to the President and Congress on their progress toward these objectives.

■ In Chapter 7 we examine **the rulemaking process** and suggest that agencies be given more flexibility to select the procedure that best fits the problem at hand from a fixed menu that would include approaches of varying formality (see pages 105–112). We also discuss ideas for streamlining the informal rulemaking process.

■ In Chapter 8 we discuss the potential that **nongovernmental organizations** possess for facilitating sound environmental and health regulatory policies (see pages 113–116).

2

THE EXECUTIVE OFFICE OF THE PRESIDENT: POLICY FORMULATION AND REGULATORY REVIEW

The Executive Office of the President is a logical focal point for regulatory reform. It is the only entity in the federal government that can take an expansive view of the regulatory landscape — no congressional committee commands such a sweeping perspective. For this reason presidents have traditionally relied on the Executive Office of the President (the former Bureau of the Budget in particular) to oversee the nation's regulatory apparatus.

In recent years many observers have questioned the Executive Office's effectiveness at this task. They perceived an unnecessarily high tension level between White House staff and regulators, with time, energy, and money wasted on internecine warfare. They saw the institutional infrastructure of the Presidency engaged in micromanagement of technical details of rules prepared by expert agencies. And they chafed at the image of a White House that seemed to be able to promote consistency within the Executive Branch only by picking up mistakes its agencies leave behind.

In this section we explore the potential of the White House to play a more constructive and proactive role in regulatory policymaking. We stress the need for the President to appoint regulators who share the President's views on regulatory policy. The President must be able to track and understand major rules and should have access to documentation of the impacts of these rules. We believe that the President should use this information to work with Congress to produce better statutes where indicated and to provide broad guidance to presidential appointees in the exercise of their delegated authority. We acknowledge that fragmentation within our democratic government has traditionally served well as a check on arbitrariness and excessive accumulation of power, and we do not seek to centralize regulatory decision making in the Executive Office. Nevertheless, it is clear that the nation's regulatory bureaucracy is too large and the challenges it faces are too great to rely on a *fully* decentralized framework for decision making. The President must at least be able to define the contours of major environmental and risk-related policy initiatives. He or she cannot do this alone.

We begin by describing the major actors within the Executive Office: the Council on Environmental Quality, the Office of Science and Technology Policy, and the Office of Information and Regulatory Affairs within the Office of Management and Budget. The next section explores what we believe are the key responsibilities of the Executive Office. After this, we present a series of organizational reforms. Finally, Executive Office regulatory review is examined in more detail. Case-by-case review has resulted in more controversy than any other Executive Office regulatory policy activity. Although we have mixed views about the utility of case-by-case review, we recognize the legitimacy of a President's wish to engage in this activity, and suggest principles by which it can be carried out more efficiently and effectively.

ROLES OF CEQ, OSTP, AND OMB

Within the Executive Office of the President, the Council on Environmental Quality (CEQ), the Office of Science and Technology Policy (OSTP), and the Office of Management and Budget (OMB) now have primary responsibility for formulating and overseeing major initiatives in the areas of environmental, health, and safety policy.

THE COUNCIL ON ENVIRONMENTAL QUALITY

CEQ, established in 1969 under the National Environmental Policy Act (NEPA), was intended to serve as the President's chief advisor on environ-

---

Box 3. Key Objectives of the National Environmental Policy Act

---

In order to carry out the policy set forth in this Act, it is the continuing responsibility of the Federal Government to use all practicable means, consistent with other essential considerations of national policy, to improve and coordinate Federal plans, functions, programs, and resources to the end that the Nation may—

- fulfill the responsibilities of each generation as trustee of the environment for succeeding generations;
- assure for all Americans safe, healthful, productive, and aesthetically and culturally pleasing surroundings;
- attain the widest range of beneficial uses of the environment without degradation, risk to health or safety, or other undesirable and unintended consequences;
- preserve important historic, cultural, and natural aspects of our national heritage, and maintain, wherever possible, an environment which supports diversity, and variety of individual choice;
- achieve a balance between population and resource use which will permit high standards of living and a wide sharing of life's amenities; and
- enhance the quality of renewable resources and approach the maximum attainable recycling of depletable resources.

Source: National Environmental Policy Act, Title I, Section 101(b).

---

mental issues. Toward this end, CEQ was directed to survey agency progress in meeting goals for environmental quality set forth in NEPA (see Box 3).

THE OFFICE OF SCIENCE AND TECHNOLOGY POLICY

The White House Office of Science and Technology Policy (OSTP) provides advice on science and technology policy to the President and serves a variety of policymaking functions. Established in 1976, OSTP is led by a director and four associate directors. The director serves simultaneously as the Assistant to the President for Science and Technology. At present, an OSTP Assistant Director for the Environment has responsibility within the office for most environmental issues.

The Federal Coordinating Council for Science, Engineering, and Technology (FCCSET), established with OSTP by the National Science and

Technology Policy, Organization, and Priorities Act of 1976, fosters the coordination of the R&D-related activities of federal departments and agencies. FCCSET's influence has varied over the past decade. It is widely credited, for example, for its work in organizing federal global climate change programs. However, OSTP's analytical capabilities are limited,[18] and actions have been taken to expand them in recent years. Recently the Critical Technologies Institute (CTI), a federally funded research and development center, was established to provide support and assistance to OSTP and FCCSET in technology policy development. CTI could play an important role in identifying and promoting the development and diffusion of environmental technologies.

THE OFFICE OF MANAGEMENT AND BUDGET

The Office of Management and Budget (OMB) was created in the 1970 reorganization of the Bureau of the Budget. The Bureau was widely respected for its analytical competence and commitment to professionalism within the highly political atmosphere of the White House. Presidents traditionally relied on it to produce sound budgets that coherently implemented presidential priorities. The new OMB was intended to build additional managerial competence into the Bureau to respond to the growing complexity and unwieldiness of the federal government, particularly administrative agencies. Since the early 1970s, OMB has helped to promote the integration of economic considerations into environmental and health regulatory policy. The Office of Information and Regulatory Affairs (OIRA), within OMB, was established by the Paperwork Reduction Act of 1980 to oversee the information-gathering activities of the federal government and to oversee the management of federal regulatory activities. Executive Order 12291, issued in 1981, has strongly influenced OIRA's mission, requiring that all regulatory initiatives include an analysis of costs and benefits and that — where the law allows — no action be taken in cases where projected benefits do not exceed costs.[19] OIRA's activities have been the subject of controversy. Critics voice objections to what they see as unnecessary interference in the activities of regulatory agencies, and supporters point to what they see as the Office's positive contributions in ensuring that economic considerations are fully incorporated into federal regulatory policies. (OIRA and its activities are considered in more detail below, in the section on the "History of Executive Office Review" (pages 48–51).

NEED TO LOOK AHEAD

With few exceptions, environmental and health policymaking in the Executive Office since the early 1970s has been reactive rather than proactive and has at times been obstructive. Policy actions have largely focused on the economic impacts of individual rules and regulatory initiatives and on preventing the promulgation of regulations that appear too costly.[20] Few initiatives have been taken to control threats to public health and the environment. In part this has been because the office has not been appropriately staffed to develop forward-looking policies and provide guidance to the executive agencies. In part, too, it has been because during the lengthy era of divided government just ended Congress tended to emphasize environmental and health protection in regulatory statutes, while the Executive Branch tended to stress the economic burden of regulation in implementing those statutes. The tensions arising from interbranch relationships and divided government are explored further in Chapter 3.

We believe that the Executive Office should work to develop coherent environmental and health policy for the President that integrates economic, energy, and related concerns into the early stages of the process. The focus for this activity should be an institutional setting in which both the benefits and the costs of regulatory activities receive attention. Joint consideration of these factors in a forward-looking context will lead to more effective policies than our present system produces.

In the remainder of this chapter we first outline the functions and capabilities for science-based regulatory policymaking that we believe should reside in the Executive Office. We next describe a possible configuration for a revitalized Office of Environmental Quality in which integrative policy options can be formulated, and we propose the creation of cabinet-level working groups to set such policies. Finally, we examine the regulatory review function and its implementation in OMB and other parts of the Executive Office.

ESSENTIAL CAPABILITIES OF THE EXECUTIVE OFFICE OF THE PRESIDENT

The organizational structure and operational procedures of the Executive Office of the President (EOP) are, within broad statutory limits, the domain of the President. Since each President operates in the context of a particular set of public mandates and personal objectives, the White House organization must be structured to fit the President's agenda.

We list here what we believe are the essential capabilities needed in the Executive Office with regard to environmental and risk-related policy-making and policy oversight (see Box 4). The components of this list should serve as criteria against which to test any proposals to reorganize the Executive Office, including those that follow in this report.

We believe that the Executive Office must have the capacity to undertake several fundamental tasks in the environmental and risk-related policy arena. Of paramount importance is the capacity to identify and analyze

---

Box 4. Essential Capabilities of the Executive Office of the President in Environmental and Risk-Related Policy Formulation and Implementation

To be effective, the Executive Office of the President (EOP) must have the capacity to

- Identify and analyze issues that require the personal attention of the President

- Develop the broad outlines of comprehensive environmental and risk-related regulatory policies that integrate environmental and health concerns into the full range of national policies, particularly economic, energy, and foreign policy

- Build legislative programs, with the assistance of departments and agencies, for consideration by Congress, and respond to legislative proposals from Congress

- Exchange views on an equal-access basis with interested parties in academia, nongovernmental organizations, the states, and industry in formulating and implementing policy

- Understand the significance of the data resulting from research, development, and monitoring programs, and incorporate this information into broad environmental and risk-related policies

- Develop global environmental policies in cooperation with other nations, and foster cooperative, international approaches to addressing and preventing the net deterioration of global ecological resources

- Communicate these policies effectively to the public, federal departments and agencies, and state governments

- Develop, with the assistance of departments and agencies, broad short-range and long-range goals for federal environmental and risk-related programs, and monitor progress in achieving these goals

- Facilitate (and eventually bring to closure) the exchange of views among federal agencies in the development of coordinated policy initiatives

issues of "presidential" significance; develop the broad outlines of governmentwide environmental and risk-related policies and monitor their implementation; and build legislative programs. To the extent practicable, the policy development process should be transparent, allowing outside scrutiny of the decision-making process.

In developing environmental and risk-reduction policies, the Executive Office should rely, whenever possible, on the analytical capabilities of departments and agencies. It should help the President to define the broad contours of the Administration's environmental and risk-related policy, but must take care to leave implementation details and day-to-day regulatory decisions to the regulatory agencies. Striking the correct balance in this regard can be difficult, and determining when and at what level to intervene in the policymaking and implementation process will always be a central challenge for the Executive Office.

The analysis and assessment function, in both the agencies and the EOP, should interact closely with but remain independent from political and policy advocacy. Without such independence, operations will often supplant policymaking, and it is essential that short-term crisis management not crowd out more sustained long-term policy deliberation.

A NEW CONFIGURATION

■ **The Executive Office of the President should expand its capacity to formulate broad environmental and risk-related policies and should better integrate these policies with other national goals.**

The need to integrate comprehensive environmental and risk-related policies with economic, energy, national security, and other policies is critical. Lack of such integration has repeatedly left environmental and risk-related regulatory agencies to clean up after the fact the polluting or otherwise risk-creating side effects of actions taken by other agencies and departments. Had policy integration been given a higher priority in the past, it is likely, for instance, that energy policy would have focused much more heavily on efficiency, and market mechanisms might have been employed to achieve environmental goals; agriculture would be less dependent on pesticides and fertilizers; and federal tax laws and regulations would have promoted a wide range of environmental objectives such as development of "low waste/no waste" technology.

■ *A focal point should be created in the Executive Office of the President for developing environmental and risk-related policy in the con-*

*text of other national policy goals (particularly economic), and for helping
federal departments and agencies to integrate sustainable development and
risk reduction objectives into their activities. By strengthening the existing
Office of Environmental Quality (OEQ) and redefining its mission, this can
be achieved without new legislation.* (On February 8, 1993, the White House
announced its intention to abolish CEQ and to replace it with an "Office
of Environmental Policy." The new Office is to be staffed at approximately
one-third the level of CEQ. It will be headed by a Deputy Assistant to the
President.)

Environmental and risk-related policymaking in recent administrations has tended to be fragmented. White House staff appeared for the
most part to view regulatory agencies as victims of tunnel vision who were
unconcerned about the costs of their activities and needed periodically to
be restrained. As a result, the White House actors who were most influential
and active in regulatory policymaking were those primarily concerned with
cost control—OIRA and the Competitiveness Council.

CEQ in its earliest incarnation was a vital institution; however, in
the past decade its effectiveness has waned, in part because recent presidents
have made only limited use of the analytical potential of the council (indeed, President Reagan reduced its staff to a skeletal level). As one scholar
of the National Environmental Policy Act put it:

> CEQ was intended to be an important and powerful arm of policy, but the
> extent of its ability to fulfill its mandate depends upon the receptivity of its
> principal client, the president. Limited by presidential priorities, CEQ has
> done what it could. . . .[21]

We believe that to make sensible environmental and risk-related
policy a President must have access to analysis and advice that integrates
his or her simultaneous concerns for protecting human and ecological health
and for maximizing economic growth. No adequate locus exists at the time
of this writing within the White House for development of such analysis
and advice. We suggest adapting OEQ to this task.

Established by the Environmental Quality Improvement Act of 1970
shortly after CEQ was created, OEQ was intended to provide staff support
to CEQ.[22] Its existing expertise and institutional memory make it an obvious base on which to build a focal point for environmental and risk-related
policymaking in the White House.

Several fundamental changes are needed to reconfigure OEQ to serve
the ends we recommend for it. First, we believe the three-member CEQ
has outlived its usefulness and should be abandoned, and its functions assumed by OEQ. The tripartite council approach has not been effective in
influencing environmental policy (perhaps in recognition of this, the Bush

Administration did not appoint two of the three statutorily permitted members of CEQ). The change we call for is consistent with a recommendation in a 1988 report by many of the nation's major environmental organizations, *Blueprint for the Environment*; this report called for a reorganization of CEQ "to turn it into a Presidential staff on the environment, headed by a single director who is highly qualified and trusted by the President."[23]

A director with rank of Assistant to the President for the Environment should head the OEQ. In this capacity the Director should lead efforts in the Executive Office to develop environmental and risk-related policy options, presenting proposals to the President and the Cabinet for their consideration. The Director should also be responsible for looking across all departments and agencies and identifying ways that federal activities can be directed toward broad environmental and risk reduction objectives identified by the President. Because the Director must broker policymaking at the cabinet level, she or he should be a broad-gauged person of considerable stature, with good access and sole loyalty to the President and Vice President, who does not have an adversarial relationship with either the environmental or business communities.

In developing policy proposals, OEQ should work to integrate environmental, energy, and economic considerations. As discussed in a previous Commission report, actions should be taken "to assure the stable and sustained functioning of a high-level mechanism concerned with linking environment, energy, and the economy."[24] The Office should also address the balance between ecological and health risk reduction. OEQ should provide the Executive Office a capability to look ahead, anticipate problems, and develop long-range strategies to respond to cross-cutting challenges that require an integrated federal response. As we have suggested earlier, as things now stand day-to-day "crisis" management too often sidetracks forward-looking deliberation in the White House.

OEQ should also work with OSTP and FCCSET to identify major research and development needs, to promote the improvement of risk assessment and risk management procedures, and to coordinate major R&D initiatives. The responsibilities of OEQ and other Executive Office entities cannot be carried out effectively without a strong staff capacity to evaluate issues and define innovative approaches to address them.

■ *The Executive Office's analytical and policymaking processes should complement and not supersede the capabilities in departments and agencies.*

The White House should develop broad policies that cut across department and agency missions. Its focus should be on integrating major domestic and foreign policy considerations with environmental and risk-related policies.

We stress in particular that OEQ's mandate should be limited to defining and periodically updating the outlines of the President's administrationwide environmental and risk-related policy. Neither OEQ nor its director should second-guess individual decisions of agency heads. By virtue of this circumscribed mission and his or her allegiance to no clientele except the President, OEQ's Director should be able to span the different interests of the Cabinet in a way that an EPA Administrator (or Secretary of the Environment) could not.

Agencies and departments should be given the freedom to develop policies specific to their missions, as long as they are consistent with the broader policies established by the White House. All departments and agencies have extensive analytical and policy planning capacities. For example, EPA's Office of Policy, Planning, and Evaluation (OPPE) is better equipped to analyze most detailed environmental policy questions than the Executive Office of the President is (or should be, given the crush of other issues the White House faces), just as FDA's Office of Planning and Evaluation is best suited to analyze specific food and drug policy issues. Consequently, individual agencies should be relied upon to develop policies within their missions and to propose broader policies for consideration by the President and the Cabinet.

If EPA becomes part of a cabinet-level Department of the Environment, the White House may rely upon a Department of the Environment with an expanded mission to think more expansively than the present EPA about approaches to achieving environmental and risk reduction objectives. Such an evolution in analytical and policymaking capacity could greatly aid the Executive Office in developing broad policies that cut across the missions of departments and agencies.

■ *Cabinet-level working groups should be established to formulate and oversee the implementation of federal policies for environmental protection and risk reduction that cut across departmental boundaries. Standing groups should be created to address persistent concerns, such as the relationships among energy, environment, and the economy.* Ad hoc *groups should be created to address challenges that can be resolved over a limited period of time.*

A central challenge in environmental policymaking is integrating the large array of policy considerations that influence the quality of the environment. Policy failures often result from a narrow perspective in planning federal programs. For example, past energy, agriculture, and defense policies have devoted inadequate attention to environmental concerns. At the same time, regulatory policies have suffered from inadequate attention to potential economic incentives that could be used to drive the nation toward environmental objectives. There is relatively little interaction, for example, between the policy-planning units of EPA and the Department of the Interior. Fostering such interactions requires either a mandate from senior agency officials or initiation of relationships at lower levels and their approval by senior officials.

Cooperative interactions among agencies with missions that potentially conflict are best initiated at the highest levels of government. For this reason we recommend the establishment of cabinet-level working groups to formulate and oversee the implementation of federal policies for environmental and risk-related regulation that cut across the missions of other agencies and departments. Such working groups could be created by the President or cabinet officers on a permanent or *ad hoc* basis. We believe, however, that working groups with a defined lifetime are preferable in many respects because they would help focus attention on critical issues and would lead to intensive efforts to develop a consensus on policy directions. More routine meetings of permanent working groups would likely result in a gradual decline in attention on the part of cabinet officials.

Coordination among environmental and risk-related agencies is best handled at the agency level, since there is great similarity of interests among these agencies and because the Executive Office has a limited capacity to coordinate agency activities. Interagency coordination is addressed in Chapter 4.

■ *The Office of Science and Technology Policy (OSTP) should play a leading role in developing environmental and risk-related policies by becoming more directly involved in policy decisions involving scientific and regulatory issues, promoting consistency in the scientific aspects of risk-based decisions, and ensuring that federal R&D programs are directed to the missions of the environmental and risk-related agencies. OSTP's work in these areas should be conducted in close cooperation with the Office of Environmental Quality.*

The scientific and technological aspects of regulatory decisions are intertwined with their legal and economic components. Strict division of labor in the Executive Office of the President—and in departments and agencies—can be a negative force in policy formulation. For example, it would be highly beneficial if White House offices worked more closely in developing guidelines for evaluating risk and for analyzing the costs and benefits of potential regulatory actions. Too often in the recent past, agencies were required to proceed in the rulemaking process based on assumptions regarding OMB and Competitiveness Council requirements, only to find after completion of the analytical basis for a regulation that some of their initial assumptions were not consistent with the preferences of the Executive Office. Similarly, as we discuss in Chapter 5, it would be beneficial if there were greater consistency across agencies in risk assessment and management procedures.

EXECUTIVE OFFICE REGULATORY REVIEW

Probably no function has come to be so closely associated with environmental and health policymaking in the Executive Office as regulatory review. Case-by-case review of agency rules has been the predominant means for imprinting presidential preferences upon regulatory policy. In this section we examine the history of Executive Office review mechanisms and the controversy that has attended them. We conclude with recommendations directed toward improving the utility and credibility of regulatory review.

HISTORY OF EXECUTIVE OFFICE REVIEW

Over the past two decades, presidents have established a series of units within the Executive Office to review major regulations in the context of their impacts on the economy and other policy concerns. President Nixon established "Quality of Life" reviews, which required agencies to submit proposed "significant" rules to the Office of Management and Budget before publication in the *Federal Register*. OMB in turn circulated rules it received to other agencies for comment. Ultimately, only EPA rules were reviewed, though the process was designed to apply to other agencies as well. OMB served primarily to facilitate communication and build consensus between EPA and other agencies. It performed few independent analyses of proposed rules.

The Ford Administration's Council on Wage and Price Stability (CWPS) reviewed proposed regulations for potential impact on inflation. EPA Quality of Life reviews persisted as well. CWPS, though controversial, eventually received congressional support in the form of an amended enabling act authorizing it to participate in rulemaking proceedings and to describe inflationary impacts it believed might accompany particular agency initiatives.

The Carter Administration's Regulatory Analysis Review Group (RARG) succeeded CWPS. Created by Executive Order 12044, RARG was made up of representatives from the Council of Economic Advisers, OMB, and major agencies. The group emphasized formal interagency review of cost-effectiveness analyses prepared by agencies rather than inflationary impact assessment. Only rules designated by agencies as major were reviewable, and only a few rules from each agency were reviewed each year. In a few instances disputes were decided by the President.

In 1981, President Reagan signed Executive Order 12291, which remains in effect today, directing agencies to assess the costs and benefits of each regulation considered, to ensure that its potential benefits outweigh its potential costs, and to select the regulatory option that maximizes the net benefit to society. Agencies must additionally prepare a formal Regulatory Impact Analysis (RIA) for each "major" rule they wish to issue.[25] As discussed earlier, the Office of Information and Regulatory Affairs in OMB is designated to review regulations and agency analyses to ensure compliance with these requirements. OIRA may prevent an agency from proceeding with a proposed or final rule until it is satisfied that its requirements have been met.

In 1985, President Reagan supplemented Executive Order 12291 with Executive Order 12498, requiring agencies to submit to OIRA an annual overview of regulatory policies and objectives and information on all significant regulatory actions contemplated or in process. Proposed agency actions that will likely be controversial, costly, or otherwise politically significant are described in the *Regulatory Program of the United States*, published annually. Agencies may not proceed with proposed regulatory actions until OIRA clears them; changes in plans require OIRA approval as well.

Executive Order 12498's stated purpose is to promote rulemaking that is consistent with the President's program. It is intended to do this by, among other things, making agency heads responsible for the content of regulatory activity from its inception (rather than only in its concluding stages in rulemaking, as Executive Order 12291 does) and by collecting major initiatives in a single document to allow input from other agencies and the public before a notice of proposed rulemaking is published.[26]

Review under Executive Orders 12291 and 12498 during the Bush Administration was augmented by sporadic secondary reviews by the Council on Competitiveness, chaired by the Vice President, and by the Office of Counsel to the President. As with OIRA review under the Reagan Administration Executive Orders, these offices could prevent a proposed rule from being issued unless a statute directed otherwise. In contrast to OIRA, however, neither of the latter offices adhered to official review criteria, though informal statements make clear that cost and political feasibility were key considerations. Although the Council on Competitiveness acknowledged a desire to operate out of public view, it assumed an increasingly high profile toward the end of the Bush Administration.[27]

ISSUES RAISED

Executive Office regulatory review has proven decidedly controversial. Proponents of the review process argue that consistent and otherwise rational decision making can be achieved only by converting the mixed currencies of regulation (such as effects on employment, availability of technological benefits, and average lifespan) to a single metric. In deciding how to translate the effects of a proposed rule into costs and benefits, agencies must face distributional aspects (that is, who wins and who loses) of regulations that might otherwise remain covert. It is argued that there is no slighting of benefits that cannot readily be converted into numbers, since agencies are permitted in their analyses to describe qualitatively any information that cannot be quantified. Moreover, its supporters see Executive Office review as a means to counter bureaucratic "tunnel vision."[28] They believe that only an overarching body without program responsibilities can ensure that decision making by the various agents of the Executive Branch is harmonious and compatible with the President's program.[29]

Critics argue that review requirements are intended primarily to impede the rulemaking process and to provide additional channels through which regulated parties can intervene. Concerns are also voiced about the economic analysis that ostensibly lies at the heart of OMB review. It is said that the multiple measurements and tradeoffs inherent in most standard-settings cannot be reduced to a single meaningful net figure. By relying on cost–benefit numbers the OMB process systematically biases decision making against regulatory action, since benefits are generally much harder to quantify than costs and may be significantly discounted in present-value estimations.[30] For instance, detractors argue, studies suggest that exposure to even small concentrations of lead decreases mental capacity and increases behavioral problems in children.[31] Yet because there is not yet a widely accepted method for quantitatively assessing the economic effect of IQ loss or behavioral problems in children, this information cannot be included in a quantitative cost–benefit analysis. Critics conclude that such minimization of the value of benefits, coupled with use of arbitrary modeling assumptions (including discount rates and the value of human life), often leads to poor decisions.

We have divergent opinions about the validity of Executive Office review of agency rulemaking. Some of us view Executive Office review of individual rules as an unnecessary additional layer of bureaucracy on an already overburdened system. Rather than enhancing presidential influence over regulation, OIRA and the Vice-President's Council on Competitiveness at best merely interpose White House staff between the Chief Executive and presidentially appointed department and agency heads. Others among us see Executive Office review as essential to facilitating coherent and cost-effective regulation by our sprawling modern bureaucracy.

We therefore neither endorse nor challenge the President's need to employ Executive Office regulatory review. However, we assert that as practiced the review process has significant flaws, and we outline below a set of principles for reform. One such suggestion is that proactive and constructive activities of the Office of Environmental Quality could replace much what the Office of Management and Budget has typically done reactively.

We believe that the key defects in the regulatory review scheme used in the past were its secrecy and unpredictability. The Executive Office for the most part stood on executive privilege and insisted that its review processes remain opaque. This inaccessibility fueled public distrust of the regulatory system. Confusion existed both within and outside government because the rules and procedures of the policymaking process were often unclear. While industry at one time seemed comfortable with the Executive Office process, some segments became critical of it, frustrated by multiple layers of review without a clear locus of authority. Indeed, in some instances the review process itself might have impeded economic growth: few in business wish to make large capital investments until it is clear that a final regulatory decision has been made. Additionally, industry participation in agency policymaking was undercut because agencies avoided use of rulemaking procedures in order to evade Executive Office review (see Chapter 7).

Finally, while we believe cost–benefit analysis can contribute to sound policymaking, we do not see value in technical micromanagement by generalists. Frequently the technical details of decisions made by presidentially appointed administrators in conjunction with scientific and technological experts, following extensive public comment, were reviewed *de novo* by individuals in the Executive Office who had limited expertise. Reviews of this kind were often counterproductive.

■ **Executive Office review of regulatory decisions made by the presidentially appointed administrators of federal agencies should consist primarily of an examination of the extent to which decisions are consistent with statutory mandates and broad Administration policies.**

Within broad statutory constraints, the approach a President takes to governing is largely a personal choice. Therefore, we do not recommend a precise mechanism for overseeing the activities of federal regulatory agencies. Nonetheless, general principles of good government should guide the executive review process in whatever form it takes.

■ The President should take care to appoint agency administrators with whom a relationship of mutual trust can be established, and the President should be able to rely on the judgment of these appointed agency administrators in implementing policies. Agency performance should be evaluated in the context of the performance of these appointees. The lines of authority for decision making in the Executive Office should be clearly defined.

- If dissatisfied with the actions or progress of federal agencies, the President should work either to modify the statutes under which they operate or to make agency management changes rather than undermine agency efforts to carry out their mandated responsibilities. In reviewing agency decisions, the Executive Office should carefully consider the statutory underpinnings of agency actions, and the bases for its decisions should be clearly articulated.

- The Executive Office of the President should be realistic about its capabilities and should not review technical scientific issues unless it has the expertise to do so. Reviewing units in the Executive Office should generally defer to the scientific and technical findings of experts in federal agencies.

- There should be a minimum of regulatory review points within the Executive Office, and the review process should be clearly described. Except for communication directly related to presidential deliberation, the executive oversight process should be open to public scrutiny.

- Economic analyses should take place chiefly at the agency level in the context of clearly stated procedural guidelines developed by the Executive Office. The substance of economic analyses undertaken by federal agencies should not be modified by the Executive Office without a compelling reason. However, the Executive Office can play an important role in assuring some consistency in agency approaches to economic analysis.

CONCLUSION

We believe that the President has a potentially excellent array of institutional support in OEQ, OMB, and OSTP with which to build sound environmental and health policy. For too long, however, this support network has remained fragmented, with different facets of environmental and health policy residing predominantly in different offices (concern for the environment in CEQ, cost sensitivity in OMB, scientific competence in OSTP). This arrangement has bred inefficiency and distrust. By linking scientific competence with concerns for both economic impacts and environmental and health quality, we believe that any President, regardless of political inclinations, can build sound policy more efficiently than under the past system. Such integrated policy-making might be supplemented by limited Executive Office regulatory review as described above.

We have thus far focused on the complex relationships within the Executive Office, while only alluding to the challenging relationships between the Executive and Congress in setting and implementing regulatory policy. In the next chapter we look more closely at interactions among the three branches of the federal government.

3
CONGRESSIONAL, EXECUTIVE, AND JUDICIAL INTERACTIONS

The complexity of federal environmental and risk-related policymaking necessitates a range of interactions among the three branches of the federal government. For the most part, these interbranch relations occur in rigid adversarial contexts such as litigation and hearings. Enhancing informal communication among Congress, the Executive, and the Judiciary on environmental and risk-related issues would help each branch develop a better understanding of the responsibilities and capabilities of the other branches and would also help generate understanding of the complex issues themselves. Improved interbranch interactions would enhance the environmental and risk-related policymaking process.

THE CONSTITUTIONAL BACKDROP TO INTERBRANCH INTERACTIONS

While the Constitution mandates a separation of powers among the executive, legislative, and judicial branches of the federal government, its provisions presume a certain level of coordination and cooperation among the branches in the development, implementation, and adjudication of public policy.

Separation of powers enables Congress, the Executive, and the Judiciary to facilitate or to impede the actions of the other branches through various checks and balances. In the executive branch, presidential vetoes or approvals of legislation, appointments to the Judiciary and Executive, rulemaking, implementation of laws, and use of other discretionary powers affect the legislative and judicial branches. In Congress, authorization, funding, and oversight of executive branch activities; confirmation or rejection of presidentially nominated executive and judicial appointees; and approval, delay, or obstruction of legislation influence the Executive and, to a lesser degree, the Judiciary. Judicial review, including determination of the constitutionality of laws and evaluation of executive branch compliance with them, affects Congress and the Executive. In addition, since the legislative and executive branches often consider past court decisions in developing and reauthorizing laws and promulgating regulations, judicial precedents can influence policy as well. Through these interactions, each branch of the federal government directly or indirectly influences the shape of public policy.

The constitutional system of checks and balances creates an inherent tension among the branches of government, and differing priorities in Congress and the Executive can lead to gridlock, regardless of the political affiliations of the parties involved. However, the Framers of the Constitution intended compromise to be the alternative to gridlock, and they envisioned interbranch cooperation as essential to effective policymaking. If one or more parties in a political debate is defiant, compromise becomes unattainable, and gridlock is likely to result. Although interbranch tension is endemic (even leaving aside partisan considerations), divided government, with different parties leading Congress and the Executive, can exacerbate existing interbranch tensions and create further obstacles to policy formation.

RISK AND UNCERTAINTY IN INTERBRANCH INTERACTION

In addition to these institutional factors, the complexity and scientific uncertainty often associated with environmental and risk-related problems can amplify the difficulty Congress and the Executive face in working together to develop policy. Where consensus exists on the magnitude of a problem and a proper approach to solving it, legislators and regulators can act swiftly and effectively to remedy the situation. However, policy is much more difficult to develop and implement where uncertainty exists over the nature of a problem itself, the viability of methods to address it, or the degree to which a problem that is expensive to solve should be alleviated.

CASE STUDY IN INTERBRANCH INTERACTION: RULEMAKING AND JUDICIAL REVIEW

Since both the legislative and executive branches interact with the Judiciary through its role as legal interpreter of statutes and regulations, effective relations with the judicial branch are an important element of successful policymaking. Because of the complex technical nature of environmental and risk-related problems, Congress often enacts legislation that defines only the boundaries of its solution, delegating the details to expert agencies. As a practical matter this can result in statutory ambiguity. Sometimes such statutes prove difficult for agencies to interpret.

For example, regulatory actions under the Federal Insecticide, Fungicide, and Rodenticide Act (FIFRA), the Toxic Substances Control Act (TSCA), and the Consumer Product Safety Act (CPSA) are based on a standard of "unreasonable risk."[32] The Clean Air Act requires that the Environmental Protection Agency (EPA) set standards with an "adequate margin of safety" to ensure public health.[33] Giving concrete meaning to such terms can prove vexing. For example, what is "unreasonable" or "adequate" in the context of saving human lives? Is one excess death per million "reasonable," or is one in ten thousand, or is zero? Implementing policy requires finding answers to difficult questions like these, which sometimes necessitate tough choices such as trade-offs between costs and lives, often under great uncertainty.

In the past, when statutory and regulatory language did not present clear answers to controversial questions, interpretation of congressional intent was often left largely to the judicial branch. In such cases, the courts frequently looked to legislative histories to determine the intent of the legislature. However, the Supreme Court's 1984 decision in *Chevron* v. *Natural Resources Defense Council* has to some degree redefined the judicial role in such circumstances.[34] In cases where statutory language is ambiguous, *Chevron* established a standard of review that counsels deference to the agency interpretation of the law, rather than legislative histories or other accounts of congressional intent, unless the court finds the agency view "unreasonable."

Although it shifted a degree of decision-making authority from the Judiciary to the Executive, *Chevron* has hardly eliminated the Judiciary's role in reviewing agency rulemakings. The 1992 ruling in *Corrosion Proof Fittings* v. *Environmental Protection Agency* illustrates that even when regulatory agencies expend significant time and resources in developing regulations, the resulting rules may not survive judicial review.[35] In this case, the Fifth Circuit Court of Appeals reviewed the asbestos ban that EPA developed under the Toxic Substances Control Act.

Before EPA promulgated its ban in 1989 on nearly all new products containing asbestos, the agency spent millions of dollars and many years compiling evidence linking asbestos to lung cancer and other diseases. This marked one of the most extensive rulemaking procedures in the agency's history. However, the court overturned the restrictions on the grounds that the agency did not explicitly consider less burdensome alternatives, as the court read TSCA's Section 6 to require. In addition, the court also cited the agency for failing to allow industry comment on revised health benefit estimates and for not fully evaluating the safety of asbestos substitutes.

The asbestos decision has provoked considerable debate, and fingers have been pointed in several directions. Regardless of whether the statute, the courts, the agency, or others should be faulted in this case, it is unsettling that that EPA could not satisfy TSCA's requirements for promulgating a single rule after a decade's effort. The case raises numerous questions, including whether the executive branch should encourage Congress to revise this legislation, and under what circumstances the agency should devote such a vast amount of time and resources to a single substance at the expense of many other pressing issues in its jurisdiction.

In another 1992 case, *American Federation of Labor and Congress of Industrial Organizations (AFL-CIO)* v. *Occupational Safety and Health Administration (OSHA)*,[36] the 11th Circuit Court of Appeals remanded OSHA's Air Contaminants Standard,[37] which covered 428 toxic substances. Both industry groups and labor unions had challenged the agency's findings on specific substances and the procedures it used in setting the multisubstance standard.

When OSHA promulgated the multisubstance standard in 1989, many hailed it as an innovative approach to dealing with a backlog of unregulated substances that would likely take many years to address on a case-by-case basis. Indeed, before the Air Contaminants Standard, OSHA had issued rules on only 24 substances since the agency's creation in 1971. The court itself acknowledged this consideration, but it determined that the language of the Occupational Safety and Health Act left it no choice in remanding the standard. As in the asbestos case, many criticized the court's ruling as a setback to effective regulation. However, the opinion suggests that a congressional amendment could provide authorization for OSHA to employ such a multistandard approach to regulating toxic substances, pointing to a possible interbranch effort to address the problem of unregulated toxic substances in the workplace.

STATUTORY INTERPRETATION, STATUTORY SPECIFICITY, AND INTERBRANCH RELATIONS

Differences in statutory interpretation can exacerbate interbranch communication difficulties. To return to the TSCA and Clean Air Act examples above, Congress and the Executive may employ different definitions of "unreasonable" or "adequate," resulting in very different policy approaches. The proper degree of statutory specificity is a difficult question. If Congress provides broad mandates and leaves specific program implementation to the agencies, friction may result if congressional expectations regarding implementation are not met. However, the executive branch may have difficulty discerning congressional intent from broad legislative instructions, leaving agencies to define what is "reasonable" or "adequate."

In recent years, Congress has often employed a strategy of writing increasingly detailed legislation on environmental and risk-related issues. Since *Chevron* held that courts would defer to agency decisions, rather than evidence of congressional intent, in the case of disagreements over the proper interpretation of ambiguous legislative mandates, Congress has responded by leaving fewer areas of its environmental and risk-related legislation subject to agency interpretation.

Congress has sometimes designed legislation to spur specific agency actions in policy implementation, rather than providing general guidelines and allowing agencies to determine how best to meet those goals. These efforts have often involved including default regulations, or "hammer provisions," which take effect if agencies fail to promulgate rules or take other action as required in the statute by a specified date. The 1990 Clean Air Act Amendments, almost seven times longer than the 1970 amendments, exemplify this apparent tendency toward increasing legislative specificity.[38]

Improved interbranch communication could also help alleviate another problem that occurs with some environmental and risk-related legislation — the ability of agencies to achieve statutory goals within specified timeframes. For example, the Clean Air Act Amendments of 1970 allowed EPA only 90 days to propose six national ambient air quality standards with adequate margins of safety to protect human health. In addition, Congress set a deadline of five years for national attainment of these standards, although evidence at the time of the act's passage suggested that air pollution in cities such as Los Angeles would take 25 years to remedy.[39] Perhaps not surprisingly, more than two decades later, numerous parts of the country remain out of compliance with the act.

While some assert that Congress needs to set optimistic forcing deadlines in order to spur agency action, improved communication between the Congress and the executive branch could foster the development of more realistic goals and milestones. Such cooperative interbranch effort could lead to the development of better environmental and risk-related policy and perhaps to faster attainment of jointly agreed-upon goals.

PROMOTING INTERBRANCH COMMUNICATION

Improved communication and better understanding among the branches on environmental and risk-related policy would prove beneficial, particularly in view of the high stakes and endemic uncertainty associated with these issues. Off-the-record communication focused on broad environmental and risk-related matters, rather than specific policy outcomes, could help each branch develop realistic expectations about the capabilities and responsibilities of the other branches.

■ **Mechanisms should be devised to promote informal communication among the branches of government with respect to environmental and risk-related issues.**

Several ongoing efforts designed to foster informal communication among the branches have proven successful. In particular, the Brookings Institution (see Box 5) and the National Health Policy Forum (see Box 6) have developed innovative branch-spanning programs to improve communication and build understanding among the branches. Through informal discussions among members of each branch, these interbranch forums have taken steps toward improving the formulation, implementation, and interpretation of public policy.

The Brookings Institution hosts an annual meeting designed to improve communication among the three branches on judicial administration issues, and the National Health Policy Forum holds frequent meetings intended to provide national health policymakers in Congress and the Executive with access to experts in a range of health-related fields. Both the Brookings Institution's seminars on the Administration of Justice and the National Health Policy Forum (NHPF) offer important lessons for future interbranch programs regarding both structure and subject matter.

Organizers of each forum stress the importance of maintaining a relatively small group of high-level participants (500 for the NHPF, with 10 to 15 individuals at a small-group session and 50 to 100 attendees at a typical large meeting; 60 for the Brookings program). Greater inclusion of lower-level staff members frequently leads to decreased senior-level participation over time, the forum planners note. The off-the-record nature of these programs is another essential element of their success, according to

Box 5. The Brookings Institution's Administration of
Justice Seminars

In 1978, the Brookings Institution initiated a program designed to improve
communication among the legislative, executive, and judicial branches on
issues related to judicial administration. The Administration of Justice seminars include representatives of Congress (House and Senate Judiciary
Committee members and chief counsels), the Judiciary (the Chief Justice
of the United States is a key participant), and the Department of Justice (including the Attorney General).

The meetings provide a forum for informal, off-the-record talks among
these high-level participants. Although the structure of the program has
evolved since its inception, currently the seminars include a maximum of
60 attendees: 15 from Congress, 15 from the Judiciary, 15 from the Department of Justice, and 15 staff members. The Brookings Institution holds the
seminars annually, but the principals attend only in alternating years, with
staff members attending on off-years. The seminars include both plenary
sessions and small-group discussions over a two-day period for the
meetings of principals and in one-day meetings for staff.

A 12- to 14-member planning committee meets six times annually to determine the agenda for the program, including discussion topics and
speakers. The planning committee makes all of its decisions consensually,
and the director of the Brookings program stresses the importance of this
decision-making method. Typically, the agenda includes about six major
issues, although past seminars have included as many as a dozen.

Overall, participants rate the interbranch program as highly successful,
and in his 1992 year-end report on the federal judiciary Chief Justice
William H. Rehnquist noted that "the Brookings Institution's Seminars on the
Administration of Justice . . . have allowed a valuable sharing of perspectives
on many of the issues that have made their way into the law."*

* William H. Rehnquist, "Chief Justice Issues 1992 Year-End Report," *The Third
Branch* 25(1) (January 1993), 1–6.

participants. Such a forum allows free exploration of a range of ideas; a more
formal setting would likely stifle much of this candid debate.

Careful selection of discussion topics is an integral part of the forum
planning process. NHPF strives to choose topics that demonstrate the potential for interbranch interaction, and forum organizers prepare substantial issue briefs on each subject under discussion to inform participants who
may not have expertise in that particular subject. The Brookings Institution
uses a planning committee that meets throughout the year to arrange the
annual event and determine topics for consideration.

The nature of the group itself that sponsors the discussion influences the success of the outcome as well. Since securing the trust of partic-

Box 6. The National Health Policy Forum

Since 1972, the National Health Policy Forum (NHPF) has served as a non-partisan, nonprofit educational institution for health policymakers in Congress, the Executive Office of the President, and the federal agencies, as well as state leaders, academics, and other health specialists from across the nation. The organization is intended to provide federal health policymakers with access to experts in academia, business, labor, consumer groups, the health professions, and other parts of government.

As health issues cut across many federal agencies and congressional committees (including such areas as veterans' affairs, agriculture, environment, and science), interbranch and intrabranch communication is an essential element of effective policy. The National Health Policy Forum allows for the exchange of ideas in an off-the-record environment designed to facilitate free discussion among senior-level participants.

The Forum was modeled after an education policy program that brought policymakers together with school principals, teachers, and other groups that their legislation directly affected. According to the founder and director of NHPF, that educational forum eventually lost its efficacy as its size increased. Thus, the NHPF director stresses the importance of maintaining a small, relatively "elite" organization in order to attract high-level policymakers, mainly senior congressional staff and agency officials.

In addition to Washington-based seminars, the Forum organizes site visits that examine national health issues from a regional perspective; these programs have helped focus attention on health care issues at the state and local levels.

In organizing Forum meetings, the NHPF staff seeks to select discussion topics that involve existing or potential interactions between the branches of government, rather than those in which a single agency or group has primary control over policy. The goal of the program is to improve the federal decision-making process on health issues and to devise better policies through increased interbranch coordination and better-informed officials.

ipants is critical to the program's success, it is important that participants perceive the organizer as an "honest broker." If participants or outsiders see the program as a lobbying effort, organizers may encounter difficulty in generating the active participation of senior officials that is central to a successful program. As an established, independent, respected organization, the Brookings Institution serves as an excellent example of an honest broker. As a nonpartisan health information dissemination program, the National Health Policy Forum has also achieved this independent status.

▪ *A forum should be created in which Members of Congress, executive branch officials, and judges can meet informally to discuss broad*

*issues raised by the interaction of science and policy in environmental and
risk-related regulation.*

A forum of this kind would help the branches develop realistic
expectations about each other's capabilities and help build understanding
on complex issues related to environmental and risk-related decision making.
It is important to stress that such a forum would not involve *policy* discussions or consensus-building efforts; rather, the effort would focus on developing better interbranch *understanding.* This distinction must be maintained
so that judges can participate in the forum while maintaining their impar-
tiality and in order to preserve the separation of powers among the branches.
Such a forum could be modeled after the Brookings Institution's Administration of Justice seminars and could also adopt key elements of the National
Health Policy Forum. The program should involve a small number of high-
level participants from each of the three branches.

The Task Force is sponsoring a pilot project to develop a forum of
this kind. High-level representatives of each branch will participate in an
informal interbranch colloquy on risk management in federal environmental
and risk-related decision making. The two-day conference will involve approximately forty participants, ten from each of the three branches plus
a small number of outside experts and Task Force staff members. A planning
committee will meet during the year to determine discussion topics and
to address other important issues. If the conference proves successful, the
Task Force hopes that this program will develop into an annual event, facilitating interbranch communications and leading to improvements in public
policy.

■ *Informal working groups at both the principal and staff levels
should be organized more frequently to foster communication between the
executive and legislative branches in developing and implementing environmental and risk-related policy.*

While congressional–executive consultation is fairly common in
developing legislation, such interbranch contact is typically less frequent
during program implementation. Informal working groups at the staff and
principal levels would prove useful in enhancing communication between
Congress and executive agencies at all stages of policy development and
implementation.

In a recent report, the National Academy of Public Administration
recommended the establishment of staff-to-staff working groups designed
to facilitate interbranch communications.[40] Such groups could help Members of Congress and their staffs stay informed of the status of regulatory
programs in their oversight jurisdictions. Congressional–executive working
groups could also inform executive agency officials and staffs about relevant
legislative and oversight actions.

Increased interbranch interactions of both staff and principals would help cultivate productive working relationships between the branches, fostering better understanding and helping build consensus on policy directions.

CONCLUSION

More effective interaction among Congress, the Executive, and the Judiciary is essential to developing better environmental and risk-related policy in a more timely fashion. While the judicial role in discussing policy is limited, judges can contribute to discussions on the administration of law and some broader issues regarding environmental and risk-related legislation and regulation. Thus, although Congress and the Executive bear the primary responsibility for developing and implementing environmental and risk-related policy, the decision-making process would benefit from periodic informal discussions on clearly defined topics between members of the Judiciary and decision makers in the legislative and executive branches.

The complexity of environmental and risk-related issues necessitates increased informal interaction between Congress and the Executive as well. Congressional–executive communication, cooperation, and coordination foster the development of sound environmental and risk-related policies and strategies for reaching agreed-upon goals. In the next part of this report, we explore the potential for greater interaction at the executive agency level.

4
INTERAGENCY COORDINATION

The agencies with primary responsibility for regulating risks from hazardous substances have mandates that overlap in some areas and leave gaps in others. Worse probably than the occasional high-profile mistake is the sum of the myriad inefficiencies and inconsistencies that result from lack of interagency communication, any one of which by itself might be considered minor. For instance, agencies build research agendas separately, collect and organize scientific data differently, and employ their own sets of assumptions to assess risks.

To some degree diversity among agencies is both beneficial and necessary. Regulatory agencies have different missions, administer different statutes, and are responsive to different constituencies. Accordingly, institutional cultures and bureaucratic procedures differ as well. It is not always obvious which points of divergence or redundancy are rational accommodations to the agencies' individual needs, and which are wasteful or counterproductive. Yet clearly a balance must be struck between uniformity and diversity.

In this chapter we review a series of interagency coordination mechanisms employed over the last 15 years and, drawing on lessons learned, recommend the creation of a new coordination body.

PAST EXPERIENCE: THE REGULATORY AGENCIES

Over the past two decades regulatory agencies have established numerous *ad hoc* coordinating groups, liaison committees, and clearinghouses. The most significant entity of this kind, in our opinion, was the Interagency Regulatory Liaison Group (IRLG), which eventually grew into the Regulatory Council.[41]

THE INTERAGENCY REGULATORY LIAISON GROUP

Organized in 1977, IRLG served as a forum for voluntary coordination and information exchange between CPSC, EPA, FDA, and OSHA. It began as a series of informal meetings between the heads of those agencies to discuss issues of mutual concern. The officials soon discovered that there were enough interagency concerns to merit a formal structure. A three-level organization emerged in which the principals continued to meet privately and a senior staff member from each agency was designated to work full time on IRLG matters. Working groups of technical personnel were established as needed to conduct substantive projects on a part-time basis. The agencies contributed to IRLG's $1 million budget according to their respective levels of funding, with the budget covering workshops, contracted services, and related items. Leadership and office facilities rotated among the agencies.

Many of the tasks IRLG attended to were mundane, yet clearly valuable. An information exchange work group attempted to standardize data identification codes and reporting requirements so that agencies could share each other's scientific findings. A research planning group helped identify the kinds and quantity of research being conducted within each agency in order to reduce duplication. Another group established uniform standards for good laboratory practice. While this sort of activity was not controversial, certain other efforts that required assistance from institutional actors who were not part of IRLG were controversial, and some were rebuffed.

For instance, the Group had hoped to coordinate budget submissions for research—doing so would increase the agencies' clout in the budgetary process and help them to influence the pattern of NIH's substantial spending on toxicology research to better reflect regulatory needs. Unfortunately, IRLG's submission of a joint research budget for 1980 is a case study in the kind of bureaucratic conflict that makes coordination difficult. OMB initially approved the joint budget because it promised to reduce waste and redundancy. OSTP, however, thought the budget was weighted too heavily towards targeted short-term research and urged that it be revised. The effort collapsed when a top official of the Department of Health, Education, and Welfare (HEW) decided that the joint budget was merely an attempt by the regulatory agencies and OMB to gain leverage over the department's budget and convinced OMB to withdraw support.

One of IRLG's better-known products was its "cancer policy," a report that attempted to outline the scientific bases that would allow inferences to be drawn about a substance's carcinogenicity from ambiguous data. Representatives from the different agencies hotly debated the report's form and contents. OSHA, for instance, was developing a cancer policy of its own that conflicted substantively with the IRLG policy. IRLG's final policy statement resulted from lengthy negotiation and was couched in treatylike language. Although presented as a scientific document, the document in fact contained a mix of policy and scientific statements. It was published in the *Federal Register* without the participation of OSHA and later republished in the *Journal of the National Cancer Institute.*

The cancer policy's effectiveness was limited, despite its publication in both a prestigious scientific journal and the federal government's forum for official announcements. Because, among other things, agency staff who had not participated in IRLG negotiations did not feel bound by the final agreement, considerable inconsistency remained in risk assessment practices in the various agencies.

IRLG also conducted a number of important joint rulemaking initiatives. For instance, the first regulatory attention given to chlorofluorocarbons (CFCs) came in the form of an IRLG joint rulemaking. Another prominent initiative was a joint rulemaking on lead, in which the agencies attempted to promulgate a regulation that would help reduce the public's total body burden of lead to an acceptable level.

THE REGULATORY COUNCIL

Toward the end of the Carter Administration, IRLG was integrated into the Regulatory Council, a regulatory-agency-coordinating entity comprised of fifteen agencies and departments in addition to the four original agencies. The council was intended to promote sensitivity to regulatory costs through voluntary coordination.[42] Its major achievement was the establishment of the Regulatory Calendar, a list of all regulations each agency was planning to issue. President Reagan abolished the Regulatory Council soon after he took office, and the Regulatory Calendar was eventually incorporated into the OMB regulatory review process as part of OMB's annual regulatory report.

PAST EXPERIENCE: THE EXECUTIVE OFFICE

The Office of Science and Technology Policy has undertaken a number of coordination initiatives. Of these, three are particularly relevant to this discussion: the "cancer principles" (which should not be confused with IRLG's "cancer policy"), the Biotechnology Science Coordinating Committee, and the Federal Coordinating Council for Science, Engineering, and Technology's Committee on Risk Assessment.

THE CANCER PRINCIPLES

An OSTP-sponsored interagency committee developed the cancer principles in response to a 1983 report, *Risk Assessment in the Federal Government: Managing the Process*, by a panel of the National Research Council (NRC).[43] The NRC report characterized risk assessment as the product of science and an admixture of science and policy they termed "science policy"[44]; it noted that agencies must make a series of assumptions about what can be inferred from each science policy issue raised in a particular risk assessment. The report found that the legitimacy of the risk assessment process is undermined if agencies vary the assumptions they use in their own risk assessments or employ different assumptions from those of other agencies assessing the same substance, in the absence of a compelling scientific rationale. It recommended that the agencies establish uniform inference guidelines to serve as a framework for integrating scientific data into risk assessments.

The OSTP group prepared the cancer principles to provide a credible statement of the state of the science upon which possible inference choices would be based. Like IRLG's cancer policy, the cancer principles were published in the *Federal Register* and republished later in a peer-reviewed scientific journal.[45] At the time of publication (in 1985) no agency had yet independently published inference guidelines. In 1986 EPA issued inference guidelines, including a classification scheme for carcinogens, which drew heavily on the background provided by OSTP's cancer principles.

THE BIOTECHNOLOGY SCIENCE COORDINATING COMMITTEE

The Biotechnology Science Coordinating Committee (BSCC) was established by OSTP in 1985 under the Federal Coordinating Council for Science, Engineering, and Technology (FCCSET).[46] It was created to help the many agencies whose purview includes biotechnology to coordinate their regulatory policies under a patchwork of statutes, none written with genetic engineering in mind. Although the document that announced the Committee's formation, the "Coordinated Framework,"[47] clarified some jurisdictional issues, much remained to be resolved.

BSCC was chaired on a rotating basis by either the Director of NIH or the Assistant Director for Biological, Behavioral, and Social Sciences of the National Science Foundation (NSF). Its other members were two assistant secretaries from the United States Department of Agriculture (USDA), FDA's Commissioner, and EPA's assistant administrators for Research and Development and for Pesticides and Toxic Substances. BSCC was chartered to identify gaps in scientific knowledge, facilitate cooperation between agencies in review of bioengineered products, and serve as a forum for sharing information and building consensus on scientific problems. Toward this end, BSCC proposed a series of definitions for organisms that would require regulatory review to provide a common basis for oversight by individual agencies. It utilized working groups to develop scientific recommendations on greenhouse containment and the conduct of small-scale field trials of bioengineered products that must be done before more releases into the environment can be permitted.[48]

A degree of controversy attended BSCC almost from its inception. Disagreements between agencies about policy questions were occasionally acrimonious; sometimes debate centered on whether questions were policy matters at all or whether they were settled scientific issues. On one occasion, BSCC's chairman communicated to OMB that other committee members disagreed with EPA on a proposed rule and that consensus was unlikely to occur. EPA subsequently found that OMB would not issue permission to publish a notice of proposed rulemaking, and the agency responded by taking the unusual step of making its draft rule available for public comment. BSCC's discontinuation followed a period during which it technically existed but no longer functioned because EPA (after the above-mentioned dispute with OMB) refused to attend its meetings.[49]

THE FCCSET COMMITTEE ON RISK ASSESSMENT

Since the late 1980s, FCCSET has played a useful role in coordinating R&D activities in federal agencies. At times its work addresses issues related to regulatory policy. For instance, FCCSET sponsored a committee on risk assessment during most of the Bush Administration. Similar to IRLG, the committee is composed of a governing board of agency officials at the deputy administrator level, as well as lower-level working groups on topics such as reproductive toxicology, neurotoxicology, and assessment of the validity and usefulness of the 1985 OSTP cancer principles.

LESSONS LEARNED

Some insights may be gleaned from examination of the coordination initiatives reviewed above. Perhaps most obvious is the determination among regulators and the Executive Office to coordinate aspects of regulatory work despite this task's inherent difficulty. Why some efforts were apparently successful and others not is less obvious, but we discern a few recurrent themes:

■ The lines between science, science policy, and policy are fuzzy and wavering. Much conflict arises over where the boundary should be drawn.

■ Coordination is necessary, but autonomy is precious: In essence, "everybody wants to coordinate, but nobody wants to be coordinated."

■ Agency participation in coordination activities must include all levels of authority; care must be taken to allocate responsibility for different activities to different levels.

■ All interested executive branch parties must have a reasonable degree of access to coordination proceedings.

IRLG's cancer policy was developed and presented as a scientific consensus statement, yet it was in fact a compilation of science and what would later come to be called science policy. OSTP's cancer principles, by contrast, were more general statements that could be plausibly labeled as "science." The IRLG cancer policy did not permeate risk assessment practice, while the OSTP cancer principles were relied upon by agencies in setting inference guidelines. We think that the difference can be ascribed in large part to the clarity brought by the NRC risk assessment report described above. OSTP recognized in 1985 that a distinction existed between science and science policy and strove to deal only with the former. The science base developed by the cancer principles allowed regulatory agencies to focus entirely on developing science policy statements, since the scientific issues had already been resolved. IRLG's effort, though pioneering, was overambitious and lacked the conceptual rigor displayed in the OSTP principles.[50]

In an analysis of BSCC, Professor Sidney Shapiro has argued that

BSCC's problems can be at least partially attributed to mixing of science-base development with policymaking. Although ostensibly established as a forum to share scientific information and develop common policies based on sound science, to an extent BSCC conflated these roles. Professor Shapiro asserts that this confusion of scientific information sharing with policy coordination led to the Committee's demise.

> The lesson to be drawn . . . is that there are two types of interagency coordination that do not mix well. The second function — requiring common policies — is inimical to the first function — exchanging information and data — because no agency will be anxious to cooperate with a process that threatens its independence. [51]

He concludes that any possibility for BSCC to function as a scientific committee disappeared when OSTP selected high-level political appointees as its members.

We agree that scientific cooperation is undermined by the atmosphere that attends policy negotiation. However, we believe that top-level policymakers *should* be involved with coordination activities that include a scientific component. Regulatory agency staff are invariably stretched thin by day-to-day demands in their own agencies. Interagency activities will always receive short shrift unless top officials make clear that it is an important priority. We can think of no more effective way for officials to communicate this priority than to participate actively themselves in aspects of the process.

The appropriate separation between science, science policy, and policy can be best achieved through a multitiered structure similar to that of IRLG or the FCCSET risk committee. Working groups of scientists, insulated from political decision makers, should be delegated authority to compile literature reviews and scientific consensus statements. These products could be used in turn by higher level groups composed of both scientific and policy officials to generate inference guidelines and similar documents. Top officials should meet periodically to develop common positions on pressing policy issues.

We acknowledge that a neat division of labor in such a complex field is hard to achieve. Our review of coordination initiatives, however, demonstrates the peril of improperly matching structure with function.

A final observation along these lines is that all interested parties within the executive branch must be given some access to the coordination process. The need for openness can be seen in the failure of IRLG's joint research budget, which resulted at least in part from a controversy between officials of HEW and OMB. No representatives of OMB or the upper echelons of HEW were invited to attend IRLG proceedings. Had they been, their concerns might have been integrated into the budget process at an earlier stage, perhaps leading to a joint budget that everyone could live with.

STRENGTHENING INTERAGENCY COORDINATION

■ **Mechanisms are needed to improve consistency in federal regulatory decision making and to facilitate interagency cooperation. One approach to meeting these needs is to establish a Regulatory Coordinating Committee comprised of the administrators of the environmental and risk-related regulatory agencies and representatives of the Executive Office of the President.**

The committee should identify problems to be addressed through the collective actions of two or more agencies. Agency staff should work to devise a consensus on ways to coordinate agency activities. Major coordination issues that cannot be resolved by staff should be reviewed by committee members. The committee should

■ Examine the relative risks posed by problems or categories of substances and attempt to identify problems that are not receiving adequate attention; ensure that major risks that cut across agency jurisdictions are being addressed and that sufficient data are developed to rank and address them appropriately; and see that relative risk rankings are regularly updated as more information becomes available. (See Chapter 5, pages 75–90, for an extended discussion of relative risk analysis.)

■ Develop and articulate a coordinated federal response to high-priority problems and set common risk reduction goals and strategies.

■ Develop methodologies and guidelines for risk assessment and risk management and promote the exchange of information among regulatory agencies. In areas where fully consistent approaches are found not to be appropriate, committee publications should explain why this is so and clearly describe the different approaches used by each agency. Committee publications should be readily available.

■ Identify research needs and the proper roles of individual agencies in meeting these needs; each agency should utilize the research strengths of other agencies to the extent possible.

The Committee should be structured to reflect the lessons learned from previous coordination efforts, as described above. We believe the Committee's center of gravity should be at the agency level, since this arrangement will likely foster a sense of *cooperation* rather than *cooption* among agencies. We recognize, however, that an administration might wish to make use of the FCCSET infrastructure for a Regulatory Coordinating Committee, and we believe such an arrangement might also work well.

In the next chapter we explore in greater detail several of the intra-agency functions mentioned above, in particular science advice, relative risk analysis, and regulatory personnel. In the last recommendation of the next chapter we call on the federal government to use its existing personnel authority to create opportunities for selected individuals to rotate among executive branch agencies, Congress, and the Executive Office of the President. The Regulatory Coordinating Committee we describe above could be staffed by individuals with such experience. The broad perspective of such individuals would enable them to respond to the differing needs of participating agencies, while working to develop a unified approach to a selected subset of issues.

5
SCIENCE, RISK, AND REGULATORY
DECISION MAKING

The fundamental problem in regulatory decision making at the agency level, as at the presidential and interagency level, is how to set priorities. It is a great challenge for science-based regulatory agencies to compare and rank individual risks and families of risks within the universe they regulate.

This difficulty can be partly ascribed to organizational fragmentation within agencies, which in turn stems at least partly from the patchwork of statutory provisions the agencies administer. More than anything else, though, its cause lies outside the agencies. Agencies are buffeted by a torrent of forces exerted by the public, the media, industry, the Executive Office of the President, legislators, and the courts. The decisions agencies make frequently seem to equal the vector sum of these forces. At one level this is good: our regulatory agencies are responsive to the people and to other government institutions. Yet, by the same token, setting priorities on a "chemical of the month" basis may result in overregulation of some hazards, underregulation of others, and reduction of agency credibility.

Our relative ignorance of the facts further complicates the task of making sound decisions about regulating risks. Data on many environmental, health, and safety risks are scarce. For example, few or no data are available on most chemicals in commerce, and data on the remainder are often insufficient for reliable risk assessment. It is also possible for reasonable people to interpret data in different ways—and this is often the case in regulatory decision making. Moreover, science by its very nature is provisional; new findings drive out old ones after a time.

Finding and organizing those data that exist is frequently difficult. Data bases in different agencies and even in different offices within agencies often cannot be readily cross-accessed.[52] This compartmentalization of information impedes efforts by top agency management to put the universe of risks they regulate into perspective. Also hampering attempts to order risks in an agency's domain sensibly is the historical preoccupation with carcinogens (and to a much lesser extent respiratory irritants and teratogens, agents which cause birth defects). Recently, agencies have begun to focus more on certain noncancer health risks and ecological risks, but further attention is needed.

As the data on environmental quality expand and improve, it will be useful to link information on trends and progress in achieving environmental objectives with the performance of federal and state regulatory programs. In its report, *Environmental Research and Development: Strengthening the Federal Infrastructure*, the Carnegie Commission discusses the importance of ensuring the proper storage of and ready access to the massive quantities of data being generated on the state of the environment. The Commission calls for a National Center for Environmental Information that "would serve as a focal point for the storage and retrieval of environmental information generated from a range of sources."[53]

In this chapter, we examine some of the means agencies use—or should use—to integrate statutory mandates with scientific findings and professional judgment in order to set a risk reduction agenda. We first look in some detail at the process known as relative risk analysis by which agencies, particularly EPA, have tried in recent years to use science and professional judgment to group risks into categories, from most pressing problems to least. Two relevant analyses are described and critiqued. We recommend that agencies strengthen their capacity to conduct sound relative risk analysis by building state-of-the-art risk data bases and experimenting with methods to integrate informed societal preferences into the relative risk process.

We next look briefly at the issue of scientific expertise for regulatory decision making. Many in the regulatory community have stressed the importance of linking experts from outside government to agency decision making through advisory committees. We agree that external science advice is extremely valuable, but we contend the pendulum may have swung too far. We recommend that agencies take deliberate steps to strengthen their internal scientific capabilities. Strong internal scientific capabilities improve the capacity of an agency to make use of external advice.

Finally, we recommend that the federal government use existing personnel authority to broaden the experiential and academic base of permanent agency staff through rotation among the branches and sabbaticals in universities and nongovernmental organizations. Science-based regulation is one of the most complex and inherently multidisciplinary endeavors in government, as our discussion on relative risk suggests. All three branches of government are actively involved in most regulatory decisions. High-quality personnel with diverse experience and education are essential if the contributions of the countless specialists involved in science-based regulation are to be successfully integrated into coherent policymaking and implementation.

RELATIVE RISK ANALYSIS

■ **Agencies should place problems in broad risk categories and develop strategies to address risks of high priority. To do this, each environmental and risk-related regulatory agency should develop a broad-based risk inventory. The agencies should use the inventories' output to help develop multidimensional risk rankings. The agencies should experiment with methods to integrate societal values into relative risk analyses where statutes do not supply all the value judgments necessary to rank risks. Agencies should repeat relative risk analysis initiatives periodically, readjusting the process at each iteration in light of lessons learned, new information, and progress in addressing high-priority risks.**

EPA has made substantial progress toward reaching this goal through two recent reports and their implementation. Both reports document the findings of interdisciplinary teams of experts who drew on extant scientific knowledge and risk assessment techniques (see Box 7 for an overview of risk assessment procedures and Box 8 for an evaluation of the risk assessment process) to compare the severity of risk posed by problems in the agency's domain.

"UNFINISHED BUSINESS" AND "REDUCING RISKS"

In the first report, *Unfinished Business*, a task force of senior career EPA managers and staff compared the relative risks posed by 31 residual environmental problems in four risk categories: human cancer risk, human non-

Box 7. Risk Assessment

Risk assessment is a composite of established disciplines, including toxicology, biostatistics, epidemiology, economics, and demography. The goals of risk assessment are to characterize the nature of the adverse effects and to produce quantitative estimates of one or both of the following fundamental quantities: (1) the *probability* that an individual (a hypothetical or identified person) will suffer disease or death as a result of a specified exposure to a pollutant or pollutants; and (2) the *consequences* of such an exposure to an entire population (i.e., the number of cases of disease or death).

Risk assessment can be either generic (e.g., an estimate of the number of excess annual cancers caused by all 189 hazardous air pollutants identified in the 1990 Clean Air Act Amendments) or site- and/or chemical-specific (e.g., the probability that a specified child will suffer neurological impairment as a result of exposure to lead in his household drinking water).

The regulatory process is generally thought to encompass two elements, risk assessment and risk management. The distinction between these two components is important, though controversial. Risk assessment is usually conceived as the "objective" part of the process, and risk management the subjective part. In risk assessment the analyst decides how big the problem is, while in risk management political decision makers decide what to do about the problem. The "conventional wisdom" (which some believe needs rethinking) stresses that risk management must not influence the processes and assumptions made in risk assessment, so the two functions must be kept conceptually and administratively separate.

Numerical estimates derived from risk assessment serve as inputs to several very different kinds of decisions, including (1) "acceptable risk" determinations (wherein action is taken if the risk exceeds some "bright line," which can be zero); (2) "cost–benefit" determinations, where the risks reduced by a proposed action are translated into benefits (e.g., lives saved, life-years extended), expressed in dollar amounts, and compared to the estimated costs of implementing the action and some rule of thumb regarding how much cost it is wise to incur to achieve a given level of benefit (e.g., $10 million to save one additional life); and (3) "cost-effectiveness" determinations, where the action that maximizes the amount of risk reduction (not necessarily expressed in dollar terms) per unit cost is favored.

Since at least 1983 (with the publication of the National Research Council's "Redbook"), the dominant paradigm for risk assessment has been a sequential, four-step process:

- *Hazard identification*—in which a qualitative determination is made of what kinds of adverse health or ecological effects a substance can cause. Typically, agencies have focused on cancer as the effect that drives further analysis and regulation. So, for example, a typical hazard identification for vinyl chloride released from industrial facili-

Box 7. (*continued*)

ties would involve the collection and critical analysis of short-term test-tube assays (for mutagenicity, etc.), of long-term animal assays (typically two-year rodent carcinogenicity tests), and of human epidemiologic data—either cohort studies (in which populations exposed to vinyl chloride are followed to assess whether their rates of any disease were significantly greater than those of unexposed or less-exposed populations) or case-control studies (which focus on victims of a particular disease to see whether they were significantly more likely to have been exposed to vinyl chloride than similar but disease-free individuals).

■ *Exposure assessment*—in which a determination is made of the amounts of a substance to which a hypothetical person (usually the "maximally exposed individual") and/or the total population are exposed. To return to the vinyl chloride example, this part of risk assessment would bring to bear techniques of emissions characterization (how much vinyl chloride leaves the plant in a given time?), fate-and-transport analysis (how is the chemical dispersed in the atmosphere and transformed into other compounds?), uptake analysis (how much air do people breathe, both outdoors and indoors?), and demographic analysis (how many hours per day do people spend in various locations near the plant, and how long do they reside in one locale before moving away?).

■ *Dose–response assessment*—in which an estimate is made of the probability or extent of injury at the exposure levels determined above, by quantifying the "potency" of the chemical in question. For vinyl chloride again, scientists would determine its carcinogenic potency by fitting the animal bioassay data (number of tumors produced at different exposure levels) to a mathematical model (usually one that is linear at low doses), and then transforming the resultant potency estimate for rodents into a human potency estimate through the use of a "scaling factor" (usually, a ratio of the body surface areas of the two species). Additionally, human epidemiologic data could be used to validate or supplant the animal-based potency estimate.

■ *Risk characterization*—in which the results of the above steps are integrated to describe the nature of the adverse effects and the strength of the evidence and to present one or more "risk numbers." For example, EPA might say, "This vinyl chloride plant is estimated to produce up to 3 excess cases of liver cancer every 70 years among the 100,000 people living within 1 mile of the facility" or "the maximally exposed individual faces an excess lifetime liver cancer risk of 5.4×10^{-4}."

Box 8.   Risk Assessment Assessed

Risk assessment is essentially a tool for extrapolating from scientific data to a risk number. The tool is made up of a host of assumptions, which are an admixture of science and policy. Sometimes either science or policy predominates, but it is often difficult to get a broad consensus that this is so.

A view among some in industry and elsewhere is that risk assessment systematically overestimates risk and frightens the public: as they see it, the typical risk assessment takes a trivial emission source, pretends that people are pressed up against the fenceline of the source 24 hours a day for 70 years, gauges the toxicity of the pollutant released by exposing ultrasensitive rodents to huge doses in the laboratory, and then uses the most "conservative" dose–response model to estimate a risk to humans at the low ambient exposures of interest. The view of some in environmental and public interest groups, and elsewhere, is that risk assessment may often inherently underestimate the true magnitude of the problem, by ignoring complicating but salient factors, including synergies among exposures, vast variations in susceptibility among humans, and unusual exposure pathways (e.g., inhalation of steam in showers containing volatilized chemicals from contaminated water).

Because the science underlying most risk assessment assumptions is inconclusive, arguments over whether or not an assumption is scientifically valid often distill down to debates about whether it is better to err on the side of "false positives" (if there is an error, it will more likely be a false indication of danger) or "false negatives" (if there is an error, it will more likely be a false indication of safety). Those who might be harmed by the substance being assessed will generally favor false positives; those who would gain from the substance will generally favor false negatives.

Two practical consequences of risk assessment's reliance on poorly substantiated assumptions are that numerical risk estimates tend to be highly uncertain and highly variable. Uncertainty refers to how likely a given estimate (expressed as a range of values) is to be true. However close a number is to being correct, it is correct only for a particular scenario—for example, average exposure level, or average individual susceptibility to the adverse effect at issue. Yet we know that exposures typically vary across space and time, and individuals probably vary widely in their susceptibility to different toxicants. Thus, any statement that "the risk is $A \times 10^{-B}$" is really a shorthand for the general truth that "we are Y% sure that the risk is no more than $A \times 10^{-B}$ for Z% of the population." If Y and Z were both very close to 100%, EPA and other agencies would not be seriously misleading themselves and the public with these shorthand statements, but that assumption is highly speculative in many cases.

Risk assessment can be most useful when those who rely on it to inform the risk management process understand its nature and its limitations, and use it accordingly. This means that decision makers must at least understand that the process is assumption- and value-laden; that they understand what assumptions were used in the assessment in question, and what values they reflect; that the risk estimate with which they work is expressed as a range, with the level of certainty that the true average is in that range quantified; and, that variability is expressed to the degree that it is known, i.e., how many and what kind of persons (e.g., children) will likely be at significantly higher or lower risk than the hypothetical average individual. Risk managers must take all these factors into account in making a decision, along with political and economic factors extrinsic to the risk assessment.

cancer risk, ecological risk, welfare risk.[54] The group ranked risks by bringing their collective professional judgment to bear on the available data, using innovative risk assessment methodology in some cases. It found that the rank order it generated differed markedly from the public's perceptions of which risks were worst. The task force discovered, moreover, that EPA and Congress had in most instances allocated resources to the problems that the public perceived as most significant, rather than to those that the experts identified as posing the highest risk.

EPA's Administrator during the Bush Administration, William K. Reilly, asked his Science Advisory Board (SAB) in 1989 to review *Unfinished Business*, and, in the light of the most recent scientific data, to assess again and compare the environmental risks EPA regulates. He asked as well that the SAB investigate strategies for reducing risks and recommend approaches for ranking and reducing risks in the future. The SAB established a 39-member Relative Risk Reduction Strategies Committee (hereafter referred to as the "risk committee"). Two subcommittees, one on ecology and one on human health, attempted to rank risks within their domains. A strategic options subcommittee summarized the multiplicity of means available to reduce risk. Each of the three subcommittees published a separate report; the major findings and recommendations of these reports were summarized in a widely distributed overview report, *Reducing Risks*.[55]

The ecology subcommittee identified areas of concern as relatively high-risk, medium-risk, and low-risk. Its report notes that gaps existed in relevant data, but that the environmental problems that it judged to be high-risk (see Box 9) "are likely to be considered high-risk even after data and analytical methodologies are improved, because the geographic scale of all four is very large (regional to global), and because the time that could be required to mitigate all four is very long, and some effects are irreversible."[56]

The health subcommittee declined to rank risks in its domain ordinally because of its view that the available data were insufficiently robust. The subcommittee did identify four problems (see Box 9) for which it said "relatively high-risk rankings were supported more firmly by the available data than they were for other health problems."[57] The subcommittee noted that better methodologies and an improved database of specific environmental toxicants could lead to a new approach to assessing human health risks.

The report of the risk committee, in addition to its rankings, made a number of recommendations that encouraged EPA to reconceptualize its mission and its approach to implementing it. The risk committee suggested that EPA, to the degree that it is legally and practically able to do so, shape and guide its programs on the basis of the severity of risks and the availability of cost-effective opportunities for reducing them. To reach this goal the risk committee called on EPA to strengthen its ecological and health

Box 9. Two Examples of Risk-Based Priorities

In 1990, the ecology subcommittee of the Environmental Protection Agency's Relative Risk Reduction Strategies Committee identified areas of concern as high-risk, medium-risk, and low-risk.

Relatively high-risk problems

- Habitat alteration and destruction
- Species extinction and overall loss of biological diversity
- Stratospheric ozone depletion
- Global climate change

Relatively medium-risk problems

- Herbicides/pesticides
- Toxics, nutrients, biochemical oxygen demand, and turbidity in surface waters
- Acid deposition
- Airborne toxics

Relatively low-risk problems

- Oil spills
- Groundwater pollution
- Radionuclides
- Acid runoff to surface waters
- Thermal pollution

The health subcommittee of the Environmental Protection Agency's Relative Risk Reduction Strategies Committee also identified areas of concern, but did not rank-order them.

- Ambient air pollutants
- Worker exposure to chemicals in industry and agriculture
- Pollution indoors
- Pollutants in drinking water

Other problem areas also involve potentially significant exposure of large populations to toxic chemicals; e.g., pesticide residues on food and toxic chemicals in consumer products. However, the data bases to support those concerns are not as robust as they are for the four areas listed above.

From U.S. Environmental Protection Agency, *Reducing Risks: Safety Priorities and Strategies for Environmental Protection* (Washington, DC: EPA, 1990), 13–14.

risk data base substantially, as well as its capability to make consistent interpretations from those data. Its report recognizes that in order to do this, EPA must cooperate and exchange information with other agencies. It also calls on EPA to provide for continual updating of its data base and for periodic reexamination its risk-based priorities.

To follow up the risk committee's recommendations, Mr. Reilly directed a number of EPA's program offices to promulgate four-year plans to focus the EPA's resources on the problems posing the highest risk, and to mirror this approach in program office budget requests. He made the use of relative risk as a decision-making tool one of his chief priorities.[58]

■ *We recommend that other risk reduction agencies conduct relative risk analyses of the type done by EPA in* Unfinished Business *and* Reducing Risks *and that both EPA and these agencies periodically update their findings and methodologies.*

We view *Unfinished Business* and *Reducing Risks* as ground-breaking enterprises, and we applaud them. We believe that other risk reduction agencies should attempt to incorporate into their own decision making and institutional culture the global perspective on risk that these reports and their implementation embody. Toward this end, we recommend that CPSC, FDA, and OSHA (and the National Institute of Occupational Safety and Health, or NIOSH) conduct similar exercises to learn how closely their expert assessments of risk correlate with public risk perceptions. We suggest that both these agencies and EPA repeat these efforts every two to four years, experimenting with scientific input from a wide range of experts from government, academia, industry, and nongovernmental organizations.

We see relative risk analysis as a promising tool for promoting scientifically sound decision making about priorities. We do not assert that relative risk analysis can by itself resolve regulatory issues; rather, it can provide a framework upon which policy may be better formulated. There is not at present a common basis for *discussing* the totality of risks each agency regulates. Without such a basis, our elected officials cannot be expected to forge a better vision of how to reduce the risks we face.

At the same time we recognize that relative risk analysis is a technique in its infancy. Much needs to be done to enhance its accuracy and credibility. In particular, we believe two components of the process must be strengthened. First, scientific data must be better collected, organized, and evaluated. As *Reducing Risks* notes, much of the existing data on health and ecological risks is not easily accessible, which undermines the effectiveness of efforts to rank risks. Second, more attention must be paid to integrating societal values into relative risk analyses. If agencies are to change their operating priorities according to the relative risk of the problems they regulate, they must be able to make broad judgments about the comparative threat of diverse problem areas. Doing so requires many value judgments, and these judgments should somehow reflect societal preferences, if the process is to be credible. In what follows we outline measures to achieve these objectives. We note here, however, that these measures will require considerable experimentation and time to implement. Agencies should view them as important supplements to ongoing risk-ranking projects like those reported in *Unfinished Business* and *Reducing Risks.*

STRENGTHENING DATA COLLECTION, ORGANIZATION, AND EVALUATION

The *sine qua non* of relative risk analysis is scientific data. Regulatory agencies clearly need to strengthen their ability to collect and array risk data. We believe agencies can take a crucial step in this direction by building comprehensive databases that are carefully formated to serve the needs of relative risk analysts. Such data bases should be used to conduct "first-order" ranking[59] of substances and problems, that is comparison of risks in similar categories. We reviewed two proposals for building a computer-based "risk inventory."[60]

The Health Subcommittee Risk Inventory Model

The health subcommittee of the EPA Science Advisory Board committee that produced *Reducing Risks* put forward the first proposal we considered. The subcommittee suggested that EPA compile a comprehensive data base of all environmental pollutants that meet both of two criteria: toxicity following exposures of environmental relevance, and evidence of widespread or intense exposure to populations or individuals. It observed that while this approach could theoretically lead to lists of hundreds or even thousands of substances, in practice it is likely that no more than a hundred pollutants could meet both criteria.

      The subcommittee recommended that information on environmental problem areas be organized in a computer data base through a matrix whose principal dimensions would be sources, agents, exposure situations, and endpoints. Each of the four elements could be ranked according to risk, as could intersections between elements (for example, "rank worst exposure situations for substance X"), thus identifying priority candidates for risk reduction. The subcommittee recommended that EPA implement its data base in small increments. Rather than address the system design as a whole, it suggests a matrix be developed for a small number of different but relatively widespread agents (connecting into existing data bases). The effort would be used as a test case from which could be gleaned design principles for a step-wise progression to a more advanced system.

The subcommittee stressed that much of the relevant data for the project it proposes resides in other agencies at the state, federal (for example, NIH, DOE, FDA, and NIOSH), and international level, as well as in the private sector. Building a credible risk inventory would require close coop-eration among these organizations. The task of building a risk inventory would in a sense never be complete, as it will need to be continually changed, expanded, and developed as experience with it is gained.

The Powers, Moore, and Upton Risk Inventory Model

In addition to the agency-specific approach proffered by the health subcom-mittee, we considered the establishment of a new freestanding governmental organization to inventory risks.[61] According to Charles Powers, John Moore, and Arthur Upton, to be successful an inventory would have to be situated outside EPA—or any regulatory agency:

> Regulatory agencies cannot be expected to divert attention from the regulatory process long enough to adequately focus on this job. And, in any event, they may have too narrow a focus (and too much cultural baggage carried over from their existing regulatory functions) to take the fresh look needed to accomplish the task.[62]

The Risk Inventory Entity (RIE) this group envisions would collect and ana-lyze all available risk data (including ecological risks) over the course of five years; they compare the scope of their proposed entity to that of the Human Genome Project.[63]

The Carnegie Risk Inventory Model

After careful deliberation we concluded that centralizing risk assessment in a single entity would be likely to diminish substantially the healthy diversity of views about risk that is found in our current multiagency system. Risk assessment is not, after all, a purely scientific enterprise. Professional judgments vary. As well, different agencies are often interested in different facets of the same hazard, and missions of federal agencies are mandated by different statutes, resulting in varied approaches to priority setting.[64]

Pragmatic considerations also militate strongly against a centralized inventory. We believe there must be close linkage between the risk assess-ment and ranking function and the operational forces of the agencies if relative risk analysis is to be other than an academic exercise. The nation's mixed experience with the National Environmental Policy Act (NEPA) provides a cautionary note here. NEPA's major shortcoming appears to have been its failure to integrate analysis into the offices where agency work is actually done. We believe similarly that creating one central entity outside the agencies to rank risks will keep rankings from penetrating the operational level.

■ *We recommend that each agency develop a risk data inventory that reflects the agency's mission and that agencies coordinate their efforts to facilitate exchange of information and interagency comparability of risk rankings.* (See Chapter 4 for a discussion of interagency coordination, including a proposal for a body that could perform the coordination function described in this recommendation.)

In recommending that inventories be located within the agencies, we did not dismiss lightly the contention that the culture and ingrained allocation of responsibilities within the regulatory agencies may impede the new thinking about risk that we advocate. We believe, however, that the needed change must occur within and between the agencies. A single new institution, that is, an RIE, would ultimately have little effect on the rest of the organizational landscape, and we do not believe that regulatory authority should be drastically redistributed.

We suggest that the agencies develop their inventories incrementally, beginning with only a few substances and problems. However, their contents should not be limited to substances that meet both of the exposure and toxicity criteria detailed earlier. Such criteria will doubtless be used in the ranking process, but should not constitute entry requirements. Ultimately, the inventories should incorporate any data that are relevant to the agencies' missions[65] and that appear to be reliable. As the inventories develop, it will be important for each agency to link its data base with data bases maintained by other organizations.[66]

We again note that this must be a gradual process. It is possible that the inventories will eventually consume enough resources to warrant their placement in separate program offices within each agency, or their ultimate consolidation into a separate independent entity. For now we believe the agencies should create a focal point within existing program offices and with dedicated staff (that is, employees whose duties are solely to develop and maintain the inventory) who will report directly to that office's director. Close liaison must be maintained with the agencies' science advisory bodies.

It is important that the inventories include ecological as well as human health effects data where indicated by agency mission. It appears that data on ecosystems could profitably be organized through a matrix with the same four principal elements that the health subcommittee suggested for health data — sources, agents, exposure situations, and endpoints.

Full assessment of many health and ecological risks requires sound atmospheric data, much of which is compiled by nonregulatory agencies, such as the National Oceanic and Atmospheric Administration (NOAA) and the National Aeronautics and Space Administration (NASA). Risk reduction agencies should link their inventories to atmospheric data bases maintained by these other agencies. One of the largest and most complex systems now under development is NASA's Earth Observing System Data and Information System (EOSDIS). Designed to process, archive, and make information readily available to users, EOSDIS will be a key component of the U.S. Global Change Research Program. Both research and regulatory agencies are likely to rely heavily on the EOSDIS program as an information resource. If the system meets expectations, it will serve as model for future interagency environmental data networks.[67]

Utility and reliability are important criteria for inclusion of data in any inventory, and chief among the indicia of reliability of scientific data would most likely be favorable peer review. Data published in peer-reviewed journals would *a priori* be acceptable for incorporation. The agencies could also establish science advisory groups to help review potentially important but unpublished data. These committees would be able to review only a fraction of the extant relevant data. They should, however, be able to develop criteria that will allow them to prescreen studies, choosing to evaluate carefully only those that seem likely to be reliable and/or to have special regulatory significance. We caution that threshold requirements for incorporating relevant data into the inventories must be considerably lower than those for journal publication. Regulatory decisions often cannot wait until journal-quality science is available, and decision makers in such situations need access to any existing data that are not patently unreliable.

Negative findings (that is, findings that show no association between observed variables) would be equal candidates for inclusion along with positive findings. Journals—and investigators—sometimes reject negative findings as uninteresting. As a result, reliable evidence that suggests that a substance does not cause a hazard often may be unpublished and otherwise unavailable. The inventories could serve as a repository for such valuable but underutilized information.

Perhaps the most critical issue each agency will face in constructing an inventory is how to organize the data within it. The process of defining an algorithm to use in arraying substances within the inventory is value-laden. The definition must reflect the preferences of agency risk managers, which should in turn reflect statutorily expressed preferences. We do not therefore prescribe a specific scheme for data categorization.

We do believe, however, that it is not sufficient to focus only on problems for which data are robust. Indeed, a central function of the inventories should be to flag as research and testing priorities substances for which preliminary data suggest a potentially serious risk. Substances with certain other profiles (such as high toxicity but relatively low exposure) might be treated as priority candidates for regulation if especially cost-effective means of controlling them are available.

The risk inventories should serve, in addition to their other functions, to facilitate early warning of unrecognized or new hazards. The agencies' first-order ranking algorithm must be capable of identifying and flagging a substance whose hazard potential changes when new results are added to their inventories.

A key to the success of each risk inventory will be its flexibility. As was noted earlier, science is a dynamic process, and this reality must be factored into the design of any mechanism through which scientific findings are to be incorporated into policymaking. In developing their inventories, we recommend that the agencies exchange experiences and ideas regularly. Such exchange might be facilitated by the coordination mechanism discussed in Chapter 4.

Sharing Risk Data

▪ *Congress and regulatory agencies should consider modifying provisions and practices directed at protection of confidential business information in order to produce a better balance between industry's need for proprietary secrecy and the need for efficient use of environmental, health, and safety data by governmental agencies, the scientific community, and the public.*

We note that a substantial impediment to data sharing and analysis, both within and among agencies, is confidential business information (CBI) provisions within certain substantive statutes designed to protect trade secrets. For example, nearly all information submitted to EPA in premanufacture notices for new chemicals is claimed as CBI under the Toxic Substances Control Act (TSCA). This information is then made available to selected staff only on a need-to-know basis.[68]

CBI provisions are costly for agencies to implement. Since under TSCA any database containing CBI becomes itself CBI, EPA must maintain separate data bases for confidential and non-confidential information. Likewise, if another federal agency needs data held by EPA but for whatever reason cannot accord the information the strict secrecy required under TSCA, the other agency must independently solicit the data. Because EPA can reveal little about CBI in its possession, other agencies may not even come to know EPA has information that would aid their research and regulatory programs. All of the above applies equally to state and international governments as well as to the nongovernmental sector. Not only are other organizations prevented from accessing CBI for their own needs, but EPA is denied valuable reviews of its CBI-based risk assessments that these other parties might provide.

One group that recently examined CBI's influence on TSCA implementation wrote that "attempts to find persons or organizations outside of [EPA's toxics office] that are making any significant use of TSCA data have proven unsuccessful."[69] Their report cited numerous examples that suggest that CBI claims under TSCA have been excessive, and recommended that legal and/or administrative reforms be made to curb these excesses.

We recognize the economic importance of protecting trade secrets and acknowledge that trade secrets must remain confidential. At the same time we have tried to show in this section and the previous one the vital need for easy access to environmental, health, and safety data by other government agencies. If the linked intraagency risk inventory system we propose in this section is to work, certain CBI provisions or their interpretation will almost surely have to be modified to allow government agencies and offices within agencies to obtain such data more easily while protecting the confidentiality of trade secrets. The same can be said for the sort of joint agency action we discuss in Chapter 4. In some instances nongovernmental organizations (NGOs) (see Chapter 8) may need access to CBI. Making this information available to NGOs should not be problematic as long as they are under contract to the government and are bound by the same requirements regarding secrecy of confidential business information as a governmental agency or department.

Communicating Information about Risk

■ *Regulatory agencies should report a range of risk estimates when assessing risk and communicating it to the public.*

How risk estimates, whether derived from an inventory or not, are conveyed to the public significantly affects the way citizens perceive those risks. Single-value risk estimates reported to the public do not provide an indication of the degree of uncertainty of risk associated with the estimate. Such numbers do not convey the conservative nature of some risk estimates. For example, most individuals are not aware that risk estimates are typically arrived at by extrapolating the information derived from high doses to the very low doses that an individual might encounter or that the number cited is often a "worst-case scenario." Communicating a range of doses provides citizens with a more realistic description of a hazard and hence results in more informed choices when the range of risks to which one is exposed is considered. For example, John Graham and his colleagues have suggested choosing an interval including "upper and lower risk estimates that a scientist believes are 80 percent likely to include the true yet unknown risk."[70] The choice of percent is arbitrary, but an interval approach such as this might give the public some sense of the certainty and confidence of a regulatory agency in the available data on a particular hazard.

VALUE INTEGRATION

Ultimately, the output of each risk inventory could and should be used by the agencies as raw material for multidimensional risk ranking. We note, however, that comparing disparate risks requires a multitude of value choices.[71] "Risk" is a complex concept. A large and growing body of liter-ature confirms the common intuition that humans factor much more into perceptions of risk than the "objective" findings of natural science.[72] Is a risk voluntary or involuntary? If an individual or group imposes a risk on others, does it listen attentively to the concerns of the risk bearer, or turn a deaf ear? Does the risk source provide benefits? Will the harm from the substance be obvious immediately after exposure, or only years later?

Beyond the generic factors that influence attitudes toward risks are what might be termed philosophical factors. Are large risks to small pop-ulations more acceptable than small risks to large populations? Which is worse, and by how much: brain damage, birth defects, cancer, or asthma? How does occupationally induced cancer in a 60-year-old compare to severe chronic asthma in a 10-year-old? How does the loss of 5 IQ points in each of 100 children compare to the eradication of 1000 species? How much less acceptable is a risk that disproportionately affects politically weak low-income or minority communities than one that affects affluent white suburbs and disadvantaged inner-city neighborhoods about equally?

An additional layer of such factors, those associated with risk "con-trollability," may become particularly salient within the context of regula-tory priority-setting. How tractable is a given problem? Can the risk be com-pletely eliminated via technological change, or can it be only partially reduced through "end-of-pipe" mechanisms? How much would it cost to control? How fast can controls be implemented?

To a large extent, these choices are embodied in the statutes that agencies administer. Congress is a focal point for the debate of environ-mental, health, and safety priorities, and legislative mandates reflect soci-etal goals and values. For a variety of reasons, Congress often decides not to regulate the "worst risks first," where the "worst" risk is understood to mean the one that will harm the most people. For example, the food statute administered by FDA places a higher regulatory burden on contaminants added to food for purposes like adding color or extending shelf life than it does on contaminants that occur naturally. In writing the law this way, Congress, presumptively reflecting a societal consensus, created a disincentive for manufacturers to add hazardous substances to the nation's food supply while not penalizing farmers for contamination they could not prevent. Legitimate legislative choices of this kind tend to be overlooked in subsequent debate of risk issues. Thus, although much of our discussion in this section is addressed to decision making within the bounds of administrative discretion, we stress the importance of fidelity to congressional intent. In many instances where agencies wish to change their regulatory priorities substantially, the correct response will be to change their lobbying priorities.[73]

Statutes, however, often do not and sometimes cannot embody all the value judgments necessary to rank risks. Agencies are left to supply many of the judgments[74] necessary to compare risks coherently.

■ *Agencies should experiment with different mechanisms for integrating societal values into the process of setting risk-based regulatory priorities.*
We believe that these value choices should not be made covertly by unaccountable "experts." There are a number of avenues through which values might properly be integrated. Prescribing a particular method is beyond the scope of our examination, but for purposes of illustration we sketch two options. We caution that whatever method an agency uses, the goal is to learn the public's "informed judgment," rather than to make the relative risk analysis process more responsive to current crises.

One possibility is for the experts to make explicit, to the extent possible, all value judgments and their relative weights in the ranking process. An agency administrator choosing to use the analysis as a basis for action would then adopt whatever judgments are made. Alternatively, the administrator might well alter the weights of different value variables so that they better reflect his or her risk management preferences. Either way, a political appointee of the President would stand accountable for the choices made.

A number of potential pitfalls are associated with this approach. It is probably impossible to capture all the policy choices that inhere in a relative risk analysis. Moreover, the results of an analysis will likely vary with the way those choices are aggregated. And making explicit certain important value judgments may seriously impede an agency administrator's ability to act. For example, it is difficult for a regulator to defend publicly the decision to trade off X lives in the present for Y lives among future generations.

Another possible way to integrate values into risk analysis would involve convening discussion groups in which citizens can agree or disagree with the conclusions of the experts *after* they have explained their rationales. Public perceptions of risk that seem unreasonable may disappear after exposure to the science underlying those risks. Other beliefs on the part of citizens may turn out to be unshakable — and, therefore, perhaps not so unreasonable. Learning from representative samples of the population which perceptions result from lack of scientific awareness and which are bedrock beliefs would seem both to promote democratic decision making and to help prevent political missteps.

Operationalizing a process of this kind so that it would both appear and *be* credible is a considerable challenge (the experiences of the Public Agenda Foundation with a similar effort are instructive — see Box 10). It would be essential that lay participants be exposed to the full range of expert opinion, be able to listen in as the experts criticize each other's positions, and (if presentations are done "live") be able to cross-examine the experts. Too formal or adversarial a proceeding might deter new thinking about risks, or might unduly tilt the discussion toward the most skilled advocate; too informal or irregular a proceeding could result in the perception that the experts are merely trying to pass their prejudices off on malleable laypersons.[75]

We envision multidimensional risk ranking as a continuing experiment. Too many elements pertain to a risk's relative significance for any process ever to yield a single "right" answer. Nonetheless, by fostering sustained dialogue between different factions of the scientific community, and between scientists and the public, relative risk analysis can help us approach that answer.

SCIENCE ADVICE

■ **Regulatory agencies should critically evaluate and take deliberate steps to improve their internal scientific capabilities and their means of integrating scientific and technological considerations into agency decision-making processes.**

A key element in setting risk-based priorities is science advice, both internal (within the agency) and external (through science advisory boards and other mechanisms). External science advisory boards serve a critically important function in providing regulatory agencies with expert advice on a wide range of issues.[76] They can also serve as a bridge between government, industry, and academia. For example, FDA recently established a new high-level science advisory board to aid in the development of research strategies and open up lines of communication between the agency and pharmaceutical companies.[77] We commend these activities and the excellent service provided by scientists, engineers, and others who serve on these boards. However, federal agencies should not rely so heavily on external advisory boards that internal scientific capabilities are neglected or are automatically assumed to be less credible than those undertaken by nongovernmental experts. High-quality internal science advice should be among an agency's highest priorities. In part, this capability is important because it allows agencies to make better use of the analyses and advice provided by external sources.

During his tenure at EPA, Administrator William Reilly asked a group of distinguished nongovernmental experts to examine the agency's internal scientific capabilities and recommend approaches to improving activities of the Office of Research and Development and the laboratories within it. This analysis resulted in thoughtful suggestions. We endorse in particular the recommendation pertaining to the development and nurturing of human resources and the establishment of a science career track at EPA, and the suggestions regarding the need to attract scientists and engineers with world-class reputations to the agency.[78]

We believe other agencies should undertake similar exercises to identify the strengths and weaknesses of their programs and to identify potential improvements. Past experience has demonstrated that regulatory decisions are only as good as the scientific information upon which they are based. The quality of the research, development, and assessment at all regulatory agencies can be substantially improved. To do so, agencies must recruit and retain first-rate scientists and engineers, provide them with state-of-the-art facilities and equipment, and give them the resources necessary to carry on research of the highest quality. Where internal capabilities are weak, bridges should be built to allow access to the best scientists and engineers in academic and nongovernmental organizations.

■ *Regulatory agencies should seek advice from other government agencies where appropriate expertise is available.*

When internal capabilities must be augmented, agency officials can frequently find expert advice within other government agencies. For example, EPA could more frequently seek the advice of experts within the National Institutes of Health, and FDA and OSHA could seek the assistance of EPA experts in evaluating environmental, health, and safety questions. Agency officials should not hesitate to seek the views of nongovernmental experts, but in doing so they should not dismiss the possibility of seeking advice from experienced individuals within government. Sharing intellectual resources across agencies promotes consistency in governmental decision making and can be more cost-effective and efficient than establishing formal external advisory bodies.

■ *Individuals with both public policy and scientific expertise should be appointed more frequently to senior positions in regulatory agencies.*

Box 10. Reducing Divergence between "Expert" and Public Beliefs about Risk: The Public Agenda Foundation Project

---

The Public Agenda Foundation, founded by Cyrus Vance, seeks to find more effective methods to present public issues so that citizens can arrive at their own more informed judgments about them. The Foundation focuses on issues where no consensus for action exists, either because of limited public understanding or because public and leadership views diverge. Public Agenda distinguishes between mass opinion—the "top-of-the-head" reactions people have to an issue regardless of how volatile or misinformed those reactions may be—and public "judgment"—the informed views people develop about an issue after they have confronted it realistically and thought seriously about the choices it entails.

In 1988 the Foundation initiated a study to discover whether the same process would work for scientific issues involving great uncertainty. Two issues were selected according to the following criteria: Leading S&T experts were concerned about the public's ability to grasp the issue, existing public opinion data suggested widespread public misunderstanding of the issue, and the policy debate on the issue was marked by conflicting S&T claims. These issues were disposal of solid waste and global warming.

The Foundation used a research method called a Citizen Review Panel in which citizens' views were examined at two points: first, at the top-of-the-head level, and second, after they had had an opportunity to learn about the issue, including its causes, possible solutions, the costs, risks, and tradeoffs associated with it, and about the areas that are marked by scientific disagreement or uncertainty.

Four hundred and two respondents from four cities were chosen to reflect a cross-section of the voting-age population. Groups met in each city for a three-hour session. Each panel completed a "pretest" questionnaire, watched a fifteen-minute video describing in a balanced way the issue of solid waste disposal, including the principal solutions, with pro and con arguments for each solution, and then broke into groups of about twelve to discuss the issue. The process was repeated for the global warming issue. Finally, panel members completed a post-test questionnaire that asked the same questions as the pretest questionnaire. To compare the public's views with those of the experts, the Foundation polled more than 1600 leading scientists using a questionnaire that contained many of the same questions asked of panel respondents (more than 400 responses were received).

The Foundation condensed its findings into eight "hypotheses":

1. Even scientifically complex issues about which there is substantial expert uncertainty can be thoughtfully considered and assessed by the public as a whole.

Box 10. *(continued)*

2. The lack of scientific knowledge is not what blocks the public from thoughtfully considering most highly scientific issues. Far more important than facts and figures is a framework within which the issue can be assessed.

3. A standard of "zero risk" is not necessary to win public confidence or assuage public concern about potentially dangerous S&T ventures.

4. Uncertainty among experts did not produce political gridlock. The public will not be paralyzed by uncertainty if certain conditions are met.

5. People deal with expert uncertainty by relating the uncertainty to their personal experience; however, such views can be tentative and subject to change given more persuasive evidence.

6. While the public's judgment about scientifically complex issues will generally be in accord with the views of most scientists, public opposition to an unpopular option may not change, no matter how much technical information people receive.

7. Leaders may mistakenly attribute public opposition to proposals that they themselves support to a lack of public understanding about the "science" of an issue when the real cause of opposition has nothing to do with scientific uncertainty.

8. The public's willingness to take the responsibility for dealing with a highly scientific issue will depend on a wide variety of factors, many of which are unrelated to science or the public's understanding of science.

In short, the Foundation found that the public will substantially change its views on many S&T-rich issues if they are exposed to a full and balanced discussion that acknowledges uncertainty and presents a framework of choices. After such exposure the Foundation's cross-section of respondents tended to come to positions that "strikingly" paralleled those of prominent scientists. Just as importantly, the Foundation found that S&T information simply cannot change some views. For instance, respondents opposed nuclear power despite evidence of its potential importance in reducing buildup of greenhouse gas emissions. Opposition seemed to rest on diverse concerns, including waste disposal problems, cost, and lack of confidence both in the people who design and manage plants and in the government's ability to regulate industry activities.

Based on John Doble and Jean Johnson, *Science and the Public: A Report in Three Volumes* (New York: Public Agenda Foundation, 1990).

Policy decisions with respect to the risk posed by hazardous substances increasingly require judgments about the quality, extent, and limits of available data; the quantitative and qualitative components of risk assessment; the biomedical and ecological aspects of environmental health and safety; and the technological feasibility of pollution prevention and remediation. Agencies should place individuals with a variety of backgrounds and experiences in senior positions. Certain senior agency positions may be better suited for an individual with a scientific background. Some offices might be better managed by a scientist who has a person with a legal background as his or her deputy or vice versa. An agency such as EPA might be well served by an administrator trained in law and a deputy with scientific credentials. Given the complexity and inherent uncertainty of risk-based decisions, there are clear advantages to seeking greater diversity and balance in senior positions. In doing so, however, managerial skills, experience, and leadership should strongly influence the selection process.

PERSONNEL

Environmental, health, and safety regulation is inherently multidisciplinary. Regulatory policy results from a dynamic interplay between politics, economics, law, ethics, and the physical and natural sciences. Within each of these fields a host of subdisciplines play important roles in regulatory decision making.

There are relatively few scholars or practitioners of regulatory policy with a truly broad view. Specialists, and fragmentation, abound. And this phenomenon extends beyond discipline to branch of government. Many congressional staff have never worked in an agency, and indeed may see the bureaucracy as something entirely foreign. The same can be said for agency staff and their perspective on Capitol Hill. Moreover, few staff of either political branch have spent time in the Judiciary.

■ **The federal government should use its existing personnel authority to create opportunities for selected individuals to rotate in the early years of their careers through environmental and risk-related regulatory agencies, Congress, the Executive Office of the President, and, in some instances, administrative offices of the Judiciary.**

The creation of such opportunities should result in a highly trained and experienced group of individuals who will bring an especially broad outlook to the regulatory process. The career protection accorded by the civil service system would insulate these individuals from political influence;

at the same time, the wide exposure to different facets of government that they would gain through their rotations should give these officials a unique perspective that will prove to be a valuable asset as their careers progress. This mix of expertise should help these civil servants eventually to become effective advisors to top policymakers.

One existing avenue for achieving this end is the Presidential Management Intern program initiated by President Carter. The program competitively selects a small number of applicants each year from schools of public policy and administration. Interns rotate among positions in the executive branch—a few also serve in congressional support agencies—for two years, after which they elect a permanent departmental home.

Selection preference for rotation opportunities among regulatory personnel should be given to those with demonstrated interest and ability in working interdisciplinarily. Rotations might usefully be longer than the two years allotted to Presidential Management Interns, and all those who participate should be required to spend some time as congressional staff. Sabbaticals might also be authorized at intervals to allow regulatory personnel to work in academic and nongovernmental institutions in order to maintain or enhance professional credentials and interact with leading nongovernmental authorities in the environmental, health, and safety fields.

We note finally that the more broadly based recommendations of the National Commission on the Public Service would help improve the conduct of science-based regulation just as they would the rest of government. We thus commend the commission's report to the interested reader.[79] Judge Stephen Breyer's paper, "Breaking the Vicious Circle: Toward Effective Risk Regulation," presents an extended discussion of the issues covered in this section.[80]

6

LONG-RANGE GOALS AND STRATEGIES
FOR REGULATORY PROGRAMS

Strategic planning is a vital but exceedingly difficult task for federal regulatory agencies. Although its importance is widely accepted, such planning tends to occupy a relatively low position among agency priorities—not intentionally but because immediate and near-term concerns often leave little time for long-term thinking. Agencies are caught in the middle of many opposing forces and a regulatory agenda that places great demands on budgets and personnel. A former EPA Administrator once compared the challenge of keeping up with the regulatory workload to "trying to perform an appendectomy while running a 100-yard dash."[81]

      Furthermore, the annual budget cycle tends to lead to myopic fiscal planning and incremental program and policy shifts. Because the budget cycle is so short, agency program managers are caught in a never-ending cycle of budget justifications, program plans, and expenditure reports. Given the immediate benefits of devoting attention to program planning in the context of the next fiscal year, agency officials have few incentives to step back from the concerns of the present and devise long-term regulatory strategies for the future. Other political time cycles reinforce the pressures toward nearsighted planning as well. The periodicity of the electoral process clearly influences the time horizon of programmatic initiatives. The President and executive branch think in terms of four and eight years, while Congress tends to plan in the context of two-year cycles (a Congress) and to some degree in four- and six-year cycles. Because of the realities of our political system and the need to achieve tangible short-term goals, elected officials and presidential appointees understandably consider initiatives in the context of relatively short time horizons. A thoroughly documented long-range plan for achieving an environmental goal may well serve the national interest but will likely generate little political capital for an individual under pressure to demonstrate his or her ability to "get things done."

ROLES OF CONGRESS AND THE EXECUTIVE

Congress and regulatory agencies have traditionally assumed a reactive rather than proactive role in addressing environmental, health, and safety risks. While it is true that events often confound expert predictions, sometimes reliable clues to the future are present, but our regulatory apparatus is not well organized to gather and assess them. In those rare instances in which Congress and federal agencies do initiate long-term planning exercises, the results typically lead to calls for substantial program shifts that are difficult to implement. Federal agencies are slow to make major changes in regulatory priorities largely because of bureaucratic inertia: budgets, personnel, and facilities become dedicated to a certain policy path, and it is difficult to change course. A senior administrator, no matter how well-intentioned or effective, may be little more than a small tug pushing an enormous tanker. He or she may be able to change the course a few degrees, but without a concerted effort on the part of many others, the agency will continue on nearly the same course.

To some extent this bureaucratic inertia is beneficial. If policies abruptly change before objectives are achieved, little is accomplished. However, it is not in the country's best interest if federal agencies become locked into achieving policy objectives that have long since fallen from the list of primary national goals. Yet, despite the difficulties and pitfalls of strategic planning, great advantages are found in looking to the future, considering long-term goals, and directing resources toward well-defined objectives.

AGENCY EXPERIENCE IN SETTING GOALS

THE ENVIRONMENTAL PROTECTION AGENCY

Several years ago, EPA officials stepped back from their immediate agenda and asked senior agency managers and experts to rank current and emerging problems according to their perception of the risks the problems posed to public health and the environment.[82] As discussed in the previous chapter of this report, the results of this effort led to the conclusion that the agency's regulatory agenda, as defined by public perceptions and statutory mandates, was not necessarily directed toward what experts considered the highest priority public health and environmental problems. The agency is now working to adjust its long-term regulatory priorities in the context of risk as assessed by experts. Statutory mandates do, of course, limit the extent to which agency officials can change regulatory priorities.

THE FOOD AND DRUG ADMINISTRATION

Like EPA, the Food and Drug Administration (FDA) periodically undertakes exercises to define regulatory objectives in the context of longer time horizons. From 1980 to 1988, FDA gained responsibility for implementing 21 new laws and amendments, while its workforce declined from 8,100 to 7,200. Concern about this trend led the agency's Office of Planning and Evaluation to undertake a "Comprehensive Needs Assessment," an extensive effort to project the resources the agency would need to accomplish its mission through 1997.[83] Through this assessment the agency concluded that in order to meet its scientific, regulatory, and enforcement responsibilities it would need to "double the size of its staff to almost 17,000 people; and triple its budget of $1.9 billion by 1997." Regardless of whether this projected need can be met, the exercise proved useful because it provided the agency an opportunity to step back from its day-to-day activities in order to assess its mission and objectives, predict future responsibilities, and define its projected resource needs. A high-level advisory panel recently evaluated FDA's research operations and found that the agency was not able to articulate effectively the nature of its "research activities, its goals, and the links between research projects and regulatory goals." FDA would benefit from improved strategic planning with respect to research and regulatory activities.[84]

THE NATIONAL INSTITUTES OF HEALTH AND THE NATIONAL SCIENCE FOUNDATION

Recently, the National Institutes of Health (NIH) and the National Science Foundation (NSF) initiated strategic planning exercises to help define the

future directions and objectives of their agencies. As NIH Director Bernadine Healy recently stated,

> [Strategic planning] must be an ongoing, living, breathing, growing process.
> This process must be capable of rapidly accommodating new scientific oppor-
> tunity and responding to . . . emergencies. The plan is not to be a blueprint;
> rather, it will serve as a compass to guide us in our course of discovery.[85]

We believe regulatory agencies would benefit greatly from the process of
developing strategic plans, and other agencies can learn much from the NIH
and NSF efforts.

FOSTERING LONG-TERM THINKING

Although federal regulatory agencies have had some success in lengthening
the time horizon of their planning efforts, many opportunities for improvement exist. Congress and the Executive Office of the President can help
catalyze these efforts. The mandates of Congress and the Office of Management and Budget heavily influence the policy planning processes of federal
agencies. With the dearth of long-range thinking in Congress and the White
House, the planning activities of regulatory agencies are limited at best and
stifled at worst. When granted an opportunity to look ahead, regulatory
agencies can be fertile sources of new ideas and can devise novel regulatory
strategies in the context of new statutory authority. We encourage Congress
and the President to look farther into the future in devising broad policy
mandates, and we recommend increased freedom for regulatory agencies
to undertake strategic planning exercises of their own.

Legislation has been introduced in the 102nd and 103rd Congresses
that would require departments and agencies to develop a "performance
standards and goals plan" for major budget expenditures.[86] The plans would
include performance indicators to track progress in achieving objectives. Eventually, plans such as these may become an integral component of budget
planning exercises.

■ **Regulatory agencies should establish specific long-term research and regulatory objectives and regularly report their progress toward achieving these
goals to the President and Congress. Congress and the President should
mandate that regulatory agencies justify annual budget and program plans
in the context of explicit long-term regulatory goals. Furthermore, Congress
should work more closely with federal and state regulatory officials and experts in nongovernmental organizations to devise realistic regulatory goals
and deadlines for meeting them.**

The Task Force on Establishing and Achieving Long-Term Goals

Regulatory agencies should articulate their long-term goals in the context of national goals and develop work plans to achieve them. The Carnegie Commission's Task Force on Establishing and Achieving Long-Term Science and Technology Goals (hereafter referred to as the Goals Task Force) has worked to devise better ways to direct the ingenuity and resources of the scientific and engineering communities to meet national objectives. A central theme of the task force's report is that federal agencies are not devoting sufficient attention to the articulation of long-term goals and consequently are not focusing resources on critical objectives. For example, the nation invests $115 billion per year to protect and restore the environment,[87] but the federal government does not have a long-range vision of how resources of this magnitude should be spent. Establishing national objectives with respect to environmental quality is of critical importance if the nation is to invest resources of this magnitude properly.

The Goals Task Force views the goal-setting process in three distinct stages: (1) *articulation* — considering the desirability and utility of setting goals, formulating draft goals and subjecting them to critical review to determine if they are realistic and achievable, and producing a clear articulation of the goal along with an explanation and justification for establishing it; (2) *introduction* — introducing the goal into the decision-making and planning processes so that it becomes an integral component of agency policy; and (3) *implementation* — working to achieve and maintain the goal over time, and reexamining the goal at suitable intervals for revalidation, complete revision, or modification.[88]

The recommendations of the Goals Task Force generally apply to regulatory planning as well. Congress often establishes deadlines for achieving environmental quality objectives, but they are frequently not met. In part, this is because the goals may be unrealistic, given available resources. A notable example (discussed above, in Chapter 3), is the Clean Air Act Amendments of 1970, which required EPA to propose national ambient air quality standards for six major pollutants 90 days from the date of enactment and to attain them in five years; these goals, twenty years later, remain unmet.

The Need for Long-Term Goals and Milestones

The process of setting goals and milestones and marshaling adequate resources to achieve them can benefit federal programs. For example, EPA has, through its pesticides program, banned 18 pesticides from use in the United States, and manufacturers have voluntarily canceled the registrations of 25 others. On the other hand, as of 1992, EPA had reregistered only two of the hundreds of older pesticides that Congress first directed the agency to reevaluate in 1972. At that time, Congress mandated that EPA complete the reregistrations within four years.[89] In 1988, Congress extended the deadline for registration to 1997. EPA's weak track record in this area is due to a variety of factors, including the lack of a commitment to an aggressive, goals-directed management program and limited and unsustained resources. For example, in 1980 EPA's pesticide program operated with 829 full-time employees. By 1985 the staff had been cut to 555; in 1992 it rose again to 1980 levels.[90] Nevertheless, a reregistration rate of one pesticide per decade suggests problems that extend beyond understaffing.

EPA's toxic substances control program could also benefit from setting long-term goals. The General Accounting Office (GAO) evaluated EPA's chemical testing program and concluded in April 1990 that the program "had made little progress. . . . It has identified for testing less than 1 percent of the more than 60,000 chemicals in the Toxic Substances Control Act (TSCA) inventory. Moreover, EPA has compiled complete test data for only six chemicals since the enactment of TSCA [in 1976] and has not finished assessing any of them."[91] In 1992, GAO reported that the chemical industry had completed testing, at EPA's direction, "on only 22 chemicals since TSCA was enacted in 1976. Of these 22 chemicals, EPA has completed its review on 16 and considered 3 of these to be particularly harmful and, therefore, candidates for regulatory action."[92] A key recommendation of the GAO report was that "the Administrator of EPA develop overall objectives for the chemical testing program and a strategy for achieving those objectives. These should identify, among other things, the universe of chemicals EPA needs to address and the pace at which it plans to address these chemicals."[93] A regulatory program such as this would benefit from the clear articulation of goals and strategies to achieve them and the development of mechanisms to monitor progress along the way.

In recent years, EPA has taken several steps to improve its chemical testing program, including greater management control of the review process, the development of an automated management tracking system, and the development of new voluntary approaches to reduce emissions of highly toxic chemicals.[94]

DEVELOPING LONG-TERM GOALS AND MILESTONES

We believe that Congress should work more closely with the regulatory agencies and experts in academia, industry, and nongovernmental organizations to establish achievable goals and deadlines. These goals should be revised periodically to account for changing circumstances. In setting goals and mandating actions by federal agencies, it is important that Congress match responsibilities with resources to ensure that objectives can be attained. Congress should articulate major goals and encourage regulatory agencies to set more specific goals and milestones in the context of these objectives. Regulatory agencies should devise work plans and secondary goals to meet congressional mandates and should monitor the progress of individuals and programs in achieving them. Monitoring progress in meeting objectives requires sound baseline information, realistic milestones, and performance standards against which achievements can be measured. Making changes such as these would prove challenging in light of the political complexities of the interactions between the executive and legislative branches. However, the value of having clearly articulated and agreed-upon goals makes greater effort in this area worthwhile.

USING LONG-RANGE REGULATORY GOALS IN AGENCY BUDGETS

The regulatory agencies attempt to carry out their missions in the context of a barrage of guidance, mandates, and demands from many policymaking corners. Numerous congressional committees and subcommittees and several offices within the Executive Office of the President, most notably the Office of Management and Budget, shape the regulatory agenda. The challenge for regulatory agencies is to weave often conflicting signals into a cohesive long-range regulatory plan and to establish short-term budget priorities in order to implement it. Well-executed research and development efforts must serve as the foundation for such plans.

We believe that Congress and the President should formalize and reinforce the long-term planning process by requiring agencies to justify budget priorities through explicit statements of how proposed activities will help achieve long-term regulatory goals.

■ **Regulatory agencies should enhance their long-range planning capabilities by strengthening the linkages between research and regulatory policymaking efforts and by undertaking policy planning exercises in the context of relative risk analyses.**

Through its Office of Policy, Planning and Evaluation (OPPE), EPA undertakes various policy planning exercises. For example, OPPE recently established an Environmental Indicators and Forecasting Branch to monitor environmental trends and to collect data to assist in long-range planning. In FDA, the Office of Planning and Evaluation undertakes anticipatory studies to help develop regulatory strategies and ensure that resources are available to implement them. To a more limited extent the Directorate of Policy within the Occupational Safety and Health Administration (OSHA) and the Office of Planning and Evaluation within the Consumer Product Safety Commission (CPSC) engage in long-range planning exercises.

■ *Regulatory agencies should strengthen their anticipatory research capabilities and establish and maintain effective linkages between these efforts and regulatory planning activities.*

The extent to which the regulatory agencies link their research and development capabilities with the planning efforts of their regulatory offices varies considerably. EPA, for example, took steps in the mid-1970s to improve connections between its Office of Research and Development and its regulatory program offices. Through a system of committees, regulatory and research officials devise research plans to ensure that R&D efforts effectively support regulatory initiatives in air, water, and hazardous waste, and other program areas.

For a brief period in the late 1970s, an Office of Strategic Assessments and Special Studies (OSASS) operated in EPA's Office of Research and Development.[95] OSASS's mission was to undertake a modest anticipatory research program to identify future environmental problems and to suggest policy responses to address them. Though the program showed promise as a mechanism to identify future environmental challenges, it had a brief life, falling victim to the budget cuts of the early 1980s. The office succeeded in developing a "Research Outlook" that evaluated pollution trends and identified research needs in the context of future challenges. However, insufficient resources and time constraints limited the scope and sophistication of the effort, weakening its impact.

We believe that each regulatory agency should establish an anticipatory research program, closely linked with its regulatory program offices, to identify emerging and potential problems as well as approaches to address them. Anticipatory research efforts should help guide the long-range planning and budget process by providing a knowledge base for future R&D and regulatory initiatives.

■ *Regulatory agencies should undertake long-term planning exercises in the context of the risk-based decision-making processes described in Chapter 5 of this report.*

In 1988, the General Accounting Office undertook a general management review of EPA and recommended that EPA incorporate risk considerations into its policy planning exercises. EPA has increasingly done so and has attempted to distinguish problems that require immediate high-priority action from those that it can address over a longer time frame. For example, it may not be wise policy to devote nearly all of an agency's program office resources to reducing by 90 percent the risk posed by 20 major hazards, if it means leaving 30 other major hazards untouched. Given finite resources, it may be better policy to work toward reducing the risk posed by all 50 major hazards by 70 percent. In making decisions of this kind, legislators and agency policymakers must balance many competing considerations against each other and make difficult trade-offs. As we noted in Chapter 5, scientific data and risk assessments derived from them constitute but one part of a much broader process.

■ *Regulatory agencies should sponsor extramural policy studies to expand and enhance agency intramural long-range planning processes.*
The wealth of talent in nongovernmental think tanks and academia could make very substantial contributions to the long-range planning efforts of regulatory agencies. Given the range, magnitude, and potential of this talent, extramural policy studies are arguably among the most underfunded of government programs. We believe that regulatory agencies should find better ways to tap this talent and should set aside funds to support contracts and grants to nongovernmental investigators and institutions. (The role of nongovernmental organizations is examined in more detail in Chapter 8.)

CONCLUSION

The long-term objectives of our environmental, health, and safety regulatory programs and the level of resources we devote to achieving them are critical considerations that merit more attention than they currently receive from agency administrators, White House officials, Members of Congress, and the nation as a whole. Agencies should develop annual or biennial budgets in the context of long-term objectives, and the success of our programs should be measured in terms of progress in achieving them. The recommendations outlined above are intended to provide federal policymakers with a framework for more systematic consideration of the future of our regulatory programs and the means of achieving national goals.

7
RULEMAKING PROCEDURES

Traditionally, administrative law has focused upon two major procedural ways in which agencies may make decisions. Sometimes agencies, acting somewhat like courts, adjudicate disputes with individual parties; at other times, acting somewhat like legislatures, they lay down rules. The Administrative Procedure Act[96] sets forth requirements that govern these two different kinds of procedures, rulemaking[97] and adjudication.[98] The Act divides rulemaking procedures themselves into two sorts, formal rulemaking[99] (for which it specifies rather detailed, trial-type procedures) and informal rulemaking[100] (for which it specifies only "notice" and "comment"). Agencies today rarely use formal rulemaking procedures because in the past the procedures often proved extraordinarily cumbersome in practice. They far more frequently set major policies through "informal rulemaking."[101]

It is important to understand that the *procedural* distinction between rulemaking and adjudication does not necessarily correspond to the *func-

tional distinction between making policy and deciding individual disputes. An agency can make policy (and highly important policy) in providing the reasons for its decision in an individual case.[102] An agency can also make policy without using either rulemaking or adjudicatory procedures. It can embody policy decisions in informal opinions, operating manuals, or even press releases.[103]

Nonetheless, rulemaking procedures have certain natural advantages as vehicles for policy formulation. Through advance notice, they alert the interested public to the problem at issue. They provide a vehicle for different groups to organize their thoughts about a matter and to present those thoughts at a specific time and in an organized way. They permit the various interested parties to comment upon the agency's and each other's proposals and comments. Through this clash of argument, they help the agency create wise policy. And they lead to a published rule, available to the public, providing guidance, setting a standard against which affected persons can fairly easily measure their conduct in advance. Such a rule potentially includes within its scope the resolution of a broad range of policy issues that might be resolvable via adjudication only through a series of cases decided piecemeal over a number of years.

Adjudicatory procedures, however, also have certain advantages in respect to policymaking. The agency can tread cautiously when it adjudicates, making policy that, in principle, is tied to the facts of the case before it, and is therefore more easily modified should future cases show the need. Moreover, the concrete nature of those facts may help to prevent the creation of policy with too broad a reach, taking inadequate account of potential differences arising out of different circumstances.[104] Nonetheless, in the past generation, the weight of scholarly opinion has tended to favor agency use of rulemaking procedures (rather than adjudicatory procedures) for determining major agency policy.[105]

The Administrative Procedure Act does not set many requirements for informal rulemaking. It insists that the agency provide "notice"[106] and give interested persons an opportunity to "comment."[107] It tells the agency that, when it publishes the resulting rule, it must set forth a "concise statement of basis and purpose."[108] Nonetheless, in interpreting these requirements since the 1960s, the courts have led agencies to develop progressively more elaborate and time-consuming procedures. Since 1970, Congress has often prescribed these and even more formal procedures for rulemaking under certain substantive statutes. Moreover, since the early 1970s, the Executive Office of the President has imposed a variety of additional analytical and reporting requirements on agency rulemaking.

Many observers, both within and outside the agencies, now believe that the cumulative weight of these constraints has led the rulemaking process to become "ossified." As a result, many agencies today tend to skirt the informal rulemaking process, turning far more frequently than in the past to methods for promulgating policies that are even less formal.[109] Agencies also seem increasingly reluctant to revisit rules when the factual or policy predicates underlying them have changed. We believe this trend is reason for significant concern. The next section describes more fully the historical reasons for this situation, and explains why it presents problems.

RULEMAKING OSSIFICATION: CAUSES AND EFFECTS

In principle, informal rulemaking involves "only" notice and comment and a "concise" agency explanation of the result. During the 1970s, however, Congress enacted many new regulatory programs (particularly those dealing with health, safety, and the environment); in doing so, it delegated broad power to agencies to promulgate important rules of great scope and economic effect; and courts, perhaps in response, began to interpret these "few" procedural requirements broadly, in an effort to guarantee a full ventilation of important issues as well as procedural fairness.[110] Thus, the "notice" requirement began to mean, not only "notice of an agency's initial proposal," but also "notice of important changes that an agency might make in its initial proposal."[111] The requirement of "comment" began to mean "meaningful" comment, which, in turn, meant an opportunity for each party to see and effectively respond to the information that the agency might use when formulating, or as a basis for, its final rule.[112] Also, the "concise" statement of basis and purpose evolved into a statement that included responses to each argument raised by any commenter, even if there were a thousand or more arguments.[113]

At the same time, the Executive itself became concerned about its ability to produce coherent, coordinated government policy, given the highly important, often related, separate policies being promulgated by many different executive branch agencies administering many different statutorily based regulatory programs. The result was an effort to achieve coordination, and consistency with general Administration policy, by bringing about higher-level review of individual agency policymaking efforts. Within each agency itself, higher-level officials would review the work of those at lower levels. The Office of Management and Budget, through its Office of Information and Regulatory Affairs, would review the proposed rules of the separate agencies.[114] Review would sometimes take place at yet higher levels, for example, the Council on Competitiveness, responsible directly to the Vice President. Central officials would review to make certain that the separate agencies had taken account of both costs and benefits, considerations of federalism, the desirability of supporting small businesses, and a host of other policies.

The result is that agency officials about to embark upon an "informal" rulemaking procedure in a complex, technical subject matter area may well face a four- or five-year rulemaking process.[115] The agency must obtain sufficient preliminary comments that the agency's notice of proposed rulemaking approximates its final result; it will then face hundreds or thousands of comments; it may then have to give each commenter a chance to answer others, in light of an information base that may change and thus may have to be continually updated. Next, the agency must write a final rule with thorough explanation and responses to criticisms; it must overcome a series of "review" hurdles within the executive branch itself (including one or more reviews at the departmental level for nonfreestanding agencies such as FDA and OSHA); and, finally, it must survive court review by judges whom the Administrative Procedure Act tells to examine the ultimate agency product (often reflecting a host of compromises) for "rationality."[116] It is not surprising that the EPA claims that informal rulemaking procedures take approximately five years to complete, that the FTC has completed only a handful of rulemaking procedures in the past decade or two, that rules once promulgated tend to remain "frozen in place," immune to change that advances in scientific knowledge would warrant, and that many agencies, such as EPA, have looked for alternative vehicles, such as negotiation with interested parties, as a way to make policy.[117]

It was not only the external legal and institutional environment that made informal rulemaking increasingly difficult. Some agencies faced serious internal obstacles, in some cases of their own making. The modern formulation of policy in the environmental, health, and safety context requires the willing collaboration of many disciplines, which in the bureaucratic context usually means many different offices or bureaus within an agency. Devising administrative mechanisms to assemble, coordinate, and organize diverse disciplines is difficult, and it is even more difficult if they are housed in or represented by different organizational units. To achieve cooperation requires determined management and continuously maintained management systems. And as the procedural responsibilities slowed the process of producing rules, it became harder to keep these systems functioning. In the early 1980s, for example, FDA largely allowed the internal management system it used to produce rules in the 1970s to collapse. Also contributing to this neglect of the management side of rulemaking was the view of the new Republican administration that new federal rules were presumptively a bad idea.

As long as informal rulemaking processes take years to complete, agencies will look for other procedural vehicles to use to promulgate policies. As previously mentioned, they may turn to adjudication and seek to set policies when deciding individual cases. Alternatively, they may embody policies in informal agency "directives," enforcement manuals, or other instructions to agency personnel. In the case of the Resource Conservation and Recovery Act (RCRA),[118] for example, there are thousands of such "directives."

The problem with setting important policies through such informal methods is that those methods may not provide an adequate opportunity for public participation in the policymaking process. Moreover, the resulting directives may be difficult for the public to find. (Indeed, because of reproduction flaws, some RCRA "directives" are illegible.[119]) Yet, serious consequences, perhaps fines or other penalties, may flow from noncompliance. Finally, many agencies avoid rulemaking because of the fear that after years of effort and the expenditure of millions of dollars, a rule will be struck down by the courts on judicial review. In some agencies, 80 percent of major rules are appealed. Some commenters argue that it is difficult to predict what factors will result in a remand[120]; agencies that believe this may thus be forced to compile huge records at great expense in order to cover every contingency.

SUGGESTIONS FOR SOLUTION

Any solution to the problems of "rulemaking ossification" must reflect an effort to balance two sets of factors. On the one hand, increased public participation and careful analysis of all aspects of a policy are desirable. On the other hand, this can lead to lengthy procedures the very length and complexity of which may defeat the desirable ends of rulemaking itself. We cannot find a perfect solution: there is no "perfect" balance. We do, however, make some suggestions that may improve the rulemaking status quo.

■ **Regulatory agencies should experiment actively with the variety of means available under existing authority to reduce rulemaking ossification. Care should be taken with all experiments to preserve adequate opportunities for analysis and public participation.**

The drafters of the Administrative Procedure Act intended it to provide tremendous flexibility to agencies. Although judicial elaboration of the Act has resulted in a series of procedural requirements that constrain agency freedom, the zone of discretion remains wide. We present a series of suggestions for using this discretion to deossify the rulemaking process.

■ *Regulatory agencies should create a "menu" of procedures, ranging from highly simple to more complex, calling for various degrees of public participation and comment, which may be subject to varying degrees of judicial review, and whose legal status may also vary. Agencies could choose the kind of procedure they believe best fits the type of policy problem at hand from among the menu's options.*

Currently, the Administrative Procedure Act provides "notice and comment" procedures applicable to agency efforts to promulgate fairly important "legislative" rules; it sets forth virtually no procedural requirements, however, in respect to agency promulgation of less important rules or directives that do not themselves have the binding status of law, as legislative rules do. It thereby encourages agencies to choose between (1) full-blown informal rulemaking procedure, and (2) no procedure.[121] The agencies, an authoritative interagency body,[122] or the Act itself, by developing a broader range of choice, would encourage agencies to permit greater public participation when creating, for instance, directives and would make the consequences of departing from full-blown informal rulemaking procedure less serious. While this new menu should include informal and perhaps formal rulemaking, if it is to be responsive to the problems described in the previous section, it must also feature a "built-down" version of informal rulemaking, and "built-up" versions of less formal policy-making modalities currently in use.

To take one example of the latter, an agency might invite a small group of perhaps thirty outside specialists to review a proposed technical operating manual at a day-long seminar—as opposed to the more typical procedure of developing the manual internally and then issuing it as a statement of agency policy without any public input.[123] The comments of that group, fewer in number than full public comment, would prove more manageable while offering at least a skeleton of dialogue between the agency and the public.

■ *Agencies should search for ways to diminish the complex time-consuming nature of the informal rulemaking process.*

Many such suggestions have been made in different forums. The following are among those that appear particularly promising.

■ Agencies could appoint "lead" commenters. If 400 potential commenters represented, say, 20 different interests, the agency could appoint 2 commenting "leaders." Others wishing to comment would ask the "leader" to reflect their points of view in his or her comments. After reviewing the leader's comments, a dissatisfied person could petition the agency for permission to submit additional comments.[124]

■ Agencies could develop two categories of response to comments, "elaborate" and "simple." The agency could sort comments into categories requiring one or the other response. As long as it acted reasonably, courts would likely defer to an agency decision to give simple responses to comments that it believes warrant them.

■ Page limits could be set on comments on a case-by-case basis.[125]

■ Agencies might try to develop "moot courts" in which to test likely judicial responses to the underlying factual or scientific basis of a final rule.

■ A mechanism like 28 U.S.C. § 1292(b) might be created to allow an agency to obtain an interlocutory appeal of the validity of a statutory interpretation upon which it intends to base a proposed regulation before the agency invests a great deal of time and money in full rulemaking.[126] Many rules are overturned by courts on the basis of an impermissible statutory interpretation, nullifying the entire rulemaking. This could be avoided if the agency had the option of certifying controlling issues of interpretation to the courts before the rulemaking began. The interlocutory appeal process has worked well for district courts in avoiding unnecessary trials and reversals on appeal where there is a controlling issue of law about which there is a substantial difference of opinion.

■ *Agencies should attempt to negotiate rules where it is possible to do so without prejudicing unrepresented third parties.*

In negotiated rulemaking (known colloquially as "reg neg," for "regulatory negotiation") representatives of various interest groups and an agency are brought together to negotiate the text of a proposed rule. The negotiation group is carefully balanced, generally including members of the regulated public, public interest groups, state and local governments, and the federal agency. If the group reaches consensus, the proposed rule is then published in the *Federal Register* for public comment just as if it had been developed in a normal rulemaking. The virtues of negotiated rulemaking have been explored elsewhere. We note that use of negotiation often saves EPA a year or two of "rulemaking" time.[127] We join the many students of the subject who advocate the use of such procedures.[128]

■ **Mechanisms should be explored to keep appropriate congressional committees informed of the interpretations made and ambiguities found by courts in the statutes that authorize rulemaking.**

For example, the Brookings Institution sponsored a well-received program in which nonpartisan analysts periodically apprised relevant committees of statutes or statutory passages that had given rise to divergent interpretations. Another possible approach is for committees with jurisdiction over regulatory statutes to devote one or two days per year to informal conferences with representatives of the agencies and the Executive Office of the President for this purpose. Efforts such as these, whether conducted by impartial NGOs or by government itself, can help promote statutory clarity. While lobbyists of all stripes offer timely and plentiful advice to congressional members and staff on what they perceive to be problems with statutes, the partiality associated with such advice sometimes leads legislators to discount it.

■ **Executive Office officials should communicate less formally, earlier, and more directly with agency officials.**

The current process of agency submission to the Executive Office of a rule, followed by Executive Office review for compliance with presidential policies, produces an adversary relationship between the agency and the Executive Office, and sometimes means delay. The causes of this relationship are complex, and may, in part, have reflected the political division previously present in the federal government. Nonetheless, we believe that increased informal consultation and discussion among agency and Executive Office staffs at an earlier stage in the process would be beneficial. Such consultation would acquaint the Executive Office staff more directly with the problems that agencies face in writing regulations in areas of scientific uncertainty. It would also help agency officials better understand the presidential policies with which they must comply. The result, we believe, would be quicker approval of more effective regulations (Chapter 2 addresses Executive Office regulatory review in more detail and presents additional recommendations for its reform).

CONCLUSION

The means that agencies employ to promulgate policy determine to a significant extent the quality of that policy and the speed with which it is implemented. Different mechanisms for policy promulgation strike different balances between efficiency on the one hand, and, on the other, opportunities for public participation (including the participation of experts), agency deliberation, and prescriptions that are easily accessible. A confluence of many factors, stemming from acts of participants in all three branches, determines this choice of means. We believe that the pattern of these choices has become worrisome, inclining increasingly toward means that unduly favor efficiency over the other values listed above. This chapter has presented a series of suggestions that we believe can help agencies strike a better balance.

8

ROLE OF NONGOVERNMENTAL ORGANIZATIONS

Thus far, the focus of this report has been on the responsibilities of the federal government in making risk-related regulatory decisions. In this chapter we discuss the important role of nongovernmental organizations in complementing and supporting the work of regulatory agencies.

As previously discussed, the regulatory apparatus has a limited capacity for evaluating environmental, health, and safety risks that cut across agency missions. Significant political and organizational barriers make such analyses a particular challenge. For example, statutory mandates limit agency activities to well-defined classes of risks, making it difficult to compare risks across agencies. Furthermore, political and other considerations, including continual crisis management demands, preclude federal agencies from performing certain kinds of analyses that could lead to innovations in the regulatory process. Consequently, regulatory policies suffer because of a lack of creative approaches to address the major environmental, health, and safety challenges facing the nation.

CONTRIBUTIONS TO POLICYMAKING

The nongovernmental sector has a proven track record in providing thoughtful nonpartisan advice for improving federal regulatory policies. We define non-governmental organizations (NGOs) as private, nonprofit organizations that contribute to the policymaking activities of the executive and legislative branches of government. Included in this definition are such organizations as the National Academy complex, policy "think tanks," such as Resources for the Future (RFF), the World Resources Institute (WRI), and the Brookings Institution. Also included are centers in academia and elsewhere that specialize in assessment and analysis of environmental issues, and organizations that both help develop policy recommendations and manage environmental problems, such as the Health Effects Institute (HEI) and Clean Sites, Incorporated (CSI). It is difficult to generalize about NGOs because of their diversity in mission and means of operating. NGOs may serve as advocates, conveners, "watchdogs" or mediators. Some strive for visibility and are active participants in the policymaking process, while others avoid publicity.[129]

In the past, NGOs with scientific and technical expertise have made major contributions to the development of environmental and regulatory policy. These contributions are seldom apparent to outside observers, as the most effective "advisor" is frequently the expert who addresses complex policy and management issues outside the public eye. William D. Carey, former Executive Officer of the American Association for the Advancement of Science (AAAS), recently described the NGO contribution to policymaking:

> Not all of [the] interfaces among NGOs and government involve high drama and headlines. . . . The grinding day-to-day headaches arising in the implementation of sensitive environmental laws and regulation, where conceptual and procedural dilemmas intersect with complications involving perception of risk, equity, and technical uncertainty, impose heavy burdens on the art and practice of public administration.[130]

It is here that some of the greatest accomplishments of NGOs can be found. The Carnegie Commission's Task Force on Nongovernmental Organizations has evaluated the role of these institutions in depth, and we commend the Commission's report on this topic to the interested reader.[131]

NGOs often serve as "bridging institutions," organizations that use novel approaches to solve problems and circumvent obstacles that have precluded or impeded action government action.[132] Clean Sites, for example, was founded in 1983 to facilitate the cleanup of hazardous waste sites throughout the nation by working to define liability among responsible parties, resolve technical disputes, and devise waste management strategies. Among other major contributions in recent years, Resources for the Future, a leading natural resources and environmental policy think tank, has pioneered the use of economic incentive-based regulatory strategies, leading to fundamental changes in federal regulatory strategies. Some NGOs, such as the Natural Resources Defense Council and the Environmental Defense Fund, both conduct analyses and vigorously advocate particular environmental and risk-related policies, often through the courts. The National Academy complex, consisting of the National Academy of Sciences, the National Academy of Engineering, the Institute of Medicine, and the National Research Council, occupies an unusual niche in the S&T NGO world as a congressionally chartered source of independent advice to the federal government. The complex has published myriad studies relevant to environmental and risk-related regulation, many extremely influential.

Nongovernmental organizations augment the capacity of government to address environmental problems by providing innovative suggestions for policy and management improvements. Their success is largely due to their relative independence, their ability to attract talented staff, and the linkages they have built to governmental entities. Perhaps the greatest weakness of the NGO–government relationship is the failure of government to take advantage of the expertise offered by these institutions.

STRENGTHENING NGO–GOVERNMENT LINKS

■ **The extensive capabilities of nongovernmental organizations should be used more frequently to evaluate the regulatory process, suggest ways to improve existing regulatory strategies, and aid federal agencies in establishing regulatory priorities. Nongovernmental policy research organizations should establish stronger ties with scientists and engineers in universities to bolster their capacities to examine issues pertaining to environmental and health risks.**

Nongovernmental policy research centers can be particularly effective in bringing together diverse groups of practitioners and scholars for sustained reflection on problems of organization and decision making in environmental and risk-related regulation. Organizations of this kind are in a unique position to convene *ad hoc* task forces to review specific organizational and decision-making regulatory issues as they arise. Ongoing research and analyses by expert staff within NGOs can supplement such periodic task force reviews. They can also provide independent evaluations of risk assessments in an effort to ensure that agency analyses conform to rigorous standards and use valid methodologies.

We encourage and support the efforts of existing institutions to improve the regulatory process. The immense environmental challenges and health risks we face in the future, coupled with existing and anticipated constraints on the federal budget, will necessitate a considerable expansion of activity in the nongovernmental sector.

Risk-related regulatory policy questions increasingly hinge on highly complex scientific questions, and NGOs must find ways to ease access to the best scientific expertise available in academic institutions. One approach to this is to have major policy research centers establish stronger linkages with universities throughout the nation in an effort to foster collaborative studies on issues with significant scientific and technical components. A center functioning as a policy research "hub" linked through a series of "spokes" to academic and other research institutions could enhance an NGO's capacity to undertake studies of a variety of technical policy issues.[133] Centers operating under this arrangement would be well-suited to examining such pressing issues as the scientific estimation of risk, risk priorities, and international efforts to reduce transboundary risks.

FUTURE NEEDS AND OPPORTUNITIES

Public confidence in the ability of governmental institutions to evaluate objectively the scientific underpinnings of complex environmental and risk-related issues has waned in recent years. Although strengthening the analytical capacity of governmental institutions should be our first priority, we believe that nongovernmental organizations will always play a critical role in the making of policy; their capabilities must be enhanced as well.

Governmental and nongovernmental organizations should develop mutually beneficial relationships to which each will bring unique skills and responsibilities. In the best of all worlds, these relationships will lead to synergies in which the two types of organization develop analytical capacities greater than the sum of their parts. Promising relationships are beginning to develop, but as a nation we are far from achieving the kinds of institutional arrangements necessary to address the diverse and highly complex scientific questions we face in the environmental, health, and safety arena.

9
CONCLUSION

The nation's regulatory agenda has changed dramatically over the past twenty years. Our regulatory agencies have already attacked many of the most opportune targets for reducing risks from hazardous substances. The risks that remain are typically complex, difficult to characterize precisely, and hard to reduce. And new problems have emerged that were at best dimly appreciated ten or twenty years ago, many bearing global consequences. Biotechnology, AIDS, greenhouse gases, and stratospheric ozone depletion are only a few of today's household words with implications regulators must face. If experience is a reliable guide, new threats lie just over the horizon.

To respond more effectively to present problems and to prepare better for future challenges, the United States must develop a more coherent, efficient, and flexible regulatory decision-making infrastructure. In this report we suggest reforms to help reach that goal.

Our examination of environmental and risk-related policymaking focuses on the role of science. Scientific data form the foundation for environmental and risk-related policymaking. Yet data are frequently limited, and what information does exist can be difficult to locate or gain access to. We believe that the regulatory system must be strongly inclined toward expanding the data base on risk: more information is better than less, as long as a framework for organizing it exists. Toward this end, we recommend that each of the agencies covered in this report develop and maintain risk inventories that consolidate and organize for easy analysis as much data as resources permit. We also call for a reevaluation of the confidential business information provisions in regulatory statutes that too often keep important health and safety information from the eyes of the regulators and the public.

While we stress the importance of sound science, we note at the same time that science's limitations mean that regulatory decision-making extends far beyond assembling data. Uncertainty permeates risk assessment and risk management; therefore, judgment permeates these processes as well. The assumptions used to fill the gap between the relatively scant data on which most assessments are based and the quantitative estimate needed from a risk assessment derive from judgment and, in turn, create uncertainty. The policymakers who employ risk assessments must then make judgments about their meaning and validity in the context of a host of conflicting political, economic, and philosophical factors that each counsel a different outcome. Moreover, few regulatory statutes offer clear guidance to risk managers on how to resolve contradictions and uncertainty.

It can be seen that the regulator's task is demanding enough in the context of a decision about a single substance or problem, yet decisions must also be made about the relative threats posed by the universe of substances and problems subject to regulation. The economic burden of regulation is so great, and the time and money available to address the many genuine environmental and health threats so limited, that hard resource allocation choices are imperative. EPA has recently taken noteworthy strides to employ science and professional judgment to rank the environmental problems within its purview. We endorse these efforts and recommend that other risk reduction agencies conduct similar experiments.

Perhaps the most striking aspect of EPA's relative risk analysis efforts is the divergence found between the experts' ranking of problems and the public's. We think that the knowledge of this divergence and the recent attempts to reduce it by increasing reliance on "scientific risk assessment" in the priority-setting process are cause for both hope and caution: hope because it is clear that in some cases it is the public's lack of a factual base for their perceptions of risk that causes them to push government to make bad decisions, and caution because in some cases the experts will be wrong and the public right. As noted above, science rarely takes decision makers more than a small part of the distance toward a decision. Intuitions and value preferences span the rest of the distance. Where members of the laity, after weighing the relevant scientific evidence, still disagree with the experts about the risk a problem poses, we believe that the experts should reconsider. We recommend that agencies experiment with mechanisms to learn the public's informed judgments about agency relative risk analyses, with a view to modifying them as appropriate.

The delicate interplay between science and judgment that makes up regulation occurs in a complex organizational ecology. Each regulatory agency, with its own mission, culture, and clientele, is beholden at different times and in different degrees to Congress, the courts, and the Executive Office of the President. Interaction among these institutions often exacerbates the inherent challenge of environmental and risk-related regulation.

To help reduce conflicts between the branches, we recommend the creation of more opportunities for informal but structured interbranch communication. Too frequently, discussions between the Executive, Congress, and the Judiciary occur only in rigid adversarial contexts like hearings. More sustained and focused off-the-record communication on broad issues (rather than on specific decisions) could help each branch develop realistic expectations about the other's capabilities and responsibilities and could provide a better basis for subsequent decision making.

Because of their independence, nongovernmental organizations (NGOs) can play an important role in facilitating informal interbranch interactions. NGOs can also serve as a bridge between the private sector and government and can complement government research and policy analysis with work of their own. Fiscal reality further enhances the value of outside expertise that is often partially funded by endowment or neutral foundations.

We believe that the three branches of government should work together to develop long-term goals and to define specific milestones along the way to achieving them. Performance must then be monitored and measured against these milestones. The absence of goals, benchmarks, and performance measurement can lead to the perception, sometimes justified, that regulatory programs are adrift among competing interests without clear purpose.

Relationships inside the executive branch present their own challenges to sound regulation. Within the Executive Office of the President, environmental and risk-related activity in recent years has centered on case-by-case review of agency rules. The Executive Office has tended to be reactive and at times obstructive rather than proactive. We suggest a more forward-looking approach. The Executive Office should provide the President with economic and policy analysis that will allow the President to set broad policy and readjust it periodically. While we recognize the President's need to oversee and review regulatory progress, we believe that the Executive Office should not try to micromanage technical details that can better be left to expert agencies. The complexity of modern risk-based regulation obliges the President to place trust in appointees to make the majority of decisions regarding policy implementation. The President can best manage the regulatory apparatus through careful appointments and good communication with appointees.

Although the White House is the only spot in the federal government that allows a sweeping overview of the regulatory landscape, the sheer number of issues it faces, most of which transcend regulation, limits its ability to ensure coherent regulatory policy. Therefore, agencies themselves must assume some responsibility for coordinating their regulatory efforts where appropriate. Currently, some problems fall between the mandates of single agencies, and others are subject to overlapping jurisdictions; thus, agencies may find themselves at cross-purposes or duplicating efforts. We recommend the creation of a regulatory coordinating committee comprised of the risk reduction agencies and representatives of the Executive Office to address these challenges.

As important as the institutional mechanisms for making policy are the legal mechanisms for promulgating it. Conventional wisdom among administrative law experts has been that the device known as "informal rule-making" is the optimal vehicle for promulgating policy. Rulemaking provides structured opportunities for public participation and generally results in clear and easily accessible policy prescriptions. Over the past decade or so, however, agencies appear increasingly to have chosen to avoid rulemaking in favor of less formal devices that provide little or no public access to the decision-making process and that result in prescriptions that are sometimes difficult or impossible to locate.

We respond to this trend with a recommendation that agencies be given a menu of policymaking modalities ranging from more to less formal, with more to less opportunity for public participation. Agencies should tailor the vehicle used to the policy being promulgated. Less formal vehicles should be accorded less or no deference on judicial review. We also set forth ideas that may help alleviate impediments to rulemaking. For instance, agencies could use moot courts to test the underlying factual or scientific basis of complex proposed rules. We recommend as well that Executive Office reviewers communicate more from the beginning of the process. A mechanism might also be created to allow an agency to obtain an interlocutory appeal of the validity of a statutory interpretation upon which it intends to base a proposed regulation before the agency invests a significant amount of time and resources in a full rulemaking. In the past, agencies have sometimes spent months or years developing regulations, only to have them rejected in either the judicial or Executive Office review process because of an incorrect fundamental premise that could have been addressed easily at the onset of the rulemaking.

The stakes are high in environmental and risk-related regulation, and the decision making takes place in a politically charged atmosphere in which distrust has been endemic. Setting regulatory policy would be an arduous task even if consensus about the facts existed, but in most regulatory controversies reasonable people can honestly disagree about the underlying "facts." Given these inherent uncertainties and the labyrinthine nature of the regulatory bureaucracy, not to mention the divided responsibility for direction and oversight involving all three branches of government, it is highly unlikely that the regulatory process can ever be fully "rationalized."

Nevertheless, the results of the recent election present an opportunity for Congress and the Executive to forge a new alliance and to modify the existing regulatory infrastructure to promote more effective regulatory policy in addressing the environmental and health challenges we face. Moreover, increasing demands on the federal budget oblige our leaders to reshape the nation's regulatory agenda. We emphasize, however, that structure can only facilitate: the quality of regulatory decisions will continue to depend primarily on people, those served by our government as well as those who serve in it.

In this report we have set forth a series of reforms that we believe will significantly enhance environmental and risk-related regulatory decision making. These recommendations, if implemented, should facilitate formulation of improved regulatory policies that will help ensure both a healthy economy and a cleaner, safer environment for future generations.

APPENDIXES

APPENDIX A
PAPERS PREPARED FOR THE TASK FORCE

Richard N. L. Andrews, "Long-Range Planning in Environmental, Health, and Safety Regulatory Agencies" (1991).

Jonathan Bender, "Selected Issues in Science, Technology, and Regulation" (1989).

Adam Finkel, "Overview of Risk Analysis" (1992).

Sheila Jasanoff, "Scientific Review and Regulatory Decision Making" (1989).

Thomas O. McGarity, "Some Thoughts on 'Deossifying' the Rulemaking Process" (1991).

Charles W. Powers, John A. Moore, Arthur C. Upton, "Improving the Coherence of Federal Regulation of Risks from Hazardous Substances" (1991).

Bruce L. R. Smith, "Use of Outside Science Advisory Bodies by Regulatory Agencies" (1992).

APPENDIX B
BIOGRAPHIES OF MEMBERS OF THE TASK FORCE

Helene L. Kaplan, Of Counsel, Skadden, Arps, Slate, Meagher & Flom, serves as counsel or trustee of many science, arts, charitable, and educational institutions. She chairs the Board of Trustees of Barnard College and is treasurer of the Association of the Bar of the City of New York. Former chairman of the Board of Trustees of Carnegie Corporation of New York, Mrs. Kaplan currently serves as a trustee of that foundation, as well as trustee of the American Museum of Natural History; Committee on Economic Development; Commonwealth Fund; J. Paul Getty Trust; John Simon Guggenheim Memorial Foundation; Institute for Advanced Study; and Mount Sinai Hospital, Medical School and Medical Center. From 1985 to 1987, she was a member of the U.S. Secretary of State's Advisory Committee on South Africa; and from 1986 to 1990, she served as a member of New York Governor Cuomo's Task Force on Life and the Law, concerned with the legal and ethical implications of advances in medical technology. Mrs. Kaplan is a director of Chemical Banking Corporation and Chemical Bank, The May Department Stores Company, Metropolitan Life Insurance Company, Mobil Corporation, and NYNEX Corporation. She is a member of the American Academy of Arts and Sciences, the American Philosophical Society, and the Council on Foreign Relations. She is a graduate of Barnard College and New York University Law School, and is the recipient of an honorary doctorate of laws from Columbia University.

Douglas M. Costle is a former administrator of the U.S. Environmental Protection Agency and former dean of Vermont Law School. Mr. Costle has also been a trial attorney in the Civil Rights Division of the U.S. Department of Justice and has served as an attorney for the U.S. Department of Commerce, Economic Development Administration. He worked as an associate with two San Francisco law firms before becoming senior staff associate to the President's Advisory Council on Executive Organization, in Washington, DC, where he played a key role in establishing the U.S. Environmental Protection Agency. Mr. Costle has served as commissioner to the Connecticut Department of Environmental Protection, as assistant director of the U.S. Congressional Budget Office, and as a fellow of the Smithsonian Institution's Woodrow Wilson International Center for Scholars. Mr. Costle has also been a visiting scholar at the Harvard School of Public Health and an adjunct lecturer in the John F. Kennedy School of Government. He is a graduate of Harvard University and the University of Chicago Law School.

Alvin L. Alm is Director and Senior Vice President of Science Applications International Corporation. Mr. Alm was previously President and CEO of Alliance Technologies Corporation and Chairman of the Board and CEO of Thermo Analytical Corporation. At Harvard University, he was Director of the Harvard Energy Security Program. Mr. Alm served within the United States Government as Deputy Administrator and Assistant Administrator of Planning and Management of the Environmental Protection Agency, Assistant Secretary for Policy and Evaluation of the Department of Energy, Staff Director of the Council on Environmental Quality and the Bureau of the Budget. Mr. Alm is Chairman of the Research Strategies Advisory Council for the EPA Science Advisory Board and Chairman of the Subcommittee on Risk Strategies of the Relative Risk Reduction Strategies Committee of the Science Advisory Board. He is a member of the Board of Directors of the Environmental Law Institute and the Center for Hazardous Materials Research. He is a graduate of the University of Denver and the Maxwell Graduate School of Syracuse University.

Richard E. Ayres is a Partner in the Washington, DC, office of the law firm of O'Melveny & Myers. Mr. Ayres was co-founder of the Natural Resources Defense Council in 1970. From 1975 to 1991, he also served as Chairman of the National Clean Air Coalition, where he played a principal role in negotiating the new Clean Air Amendments of 1990 with representatives of EPA, the White House, Congress, and industry. He served as a presidential appointee on the National Commission on Air Quality from 1979 to 1981. Mr. Ayres has had broad experience in administrative proceedings, litigation, and legislative matters. He has participated in many of the major clean air rulemaking proceedings before the U.S. Environmental Protection Agency over the past two decades. These included proceedings regarding several federal air quality (health) standards, technology standards for new electric power plants, use of tall smokestacks to disperse pollution, and pollution rights trading. Mr. Ayres successfully negotiated the largest air pollution control settlement in the nation's history, settling a multicourt federal suit involving an investment of more than $1 billion in pollution control equipment and clean fuels. He has also handled a number of cases involving interpretation of the Clean Air Act before the federal Courts of Appeal, as well as the Supreme Court of the United States. In 1981 Mr. Ayres was honored by the Yale Law Association of Washington for his outstanding service to the public interest. His practice emphasizes environmental and related energy regulatory matters.

Sheila L. Birnbaum heads the products liability department of Skadden, Arps, Slate, Meagher & Flom. Ms. Birnbaum had previously been Counsel to the firm while she was Professor of Law and Associate Dean at New York University Law School. She was Professor of Law at Fordham University School of Law and has lectured extensively across the country. She is a Council Member of the American Law Institute and the ABA's Section of Torts and Insurance Practice, and a Member of the Second Circuit Committee on the Improvement of Civil Litigation. She took her law degree at New York University, and took undergraduate and graduate degrees from Hunter College.

Stephen G. Breyer is Chief Judge of the First Judicial Circuit of the United States (Maine, Massachusetts, New Hampshire, Rhode Island and Puerto Rico). Chief Judge Breyer is a member of the Judicial Conference of the United States and has served as a member of the U.S. Sentencing Commission. He previously served as Professor at Harvard Law School and Kennedy School of Government, Chief Counsel to the U.S. Senate Judiciary Committee and Special Counsel to its Subcommittee on Administrative Practices, Assistant Special Prosecutor for the Watergate Special Prosecution Force, and Special Assistant to the Assistant Attorney General of the U.S. Department of Justice, and as a law clerk for the U.S. Supreme Court. Chief Judge Breyer is a member of the American Academy of Arts and Sciences and the American Law Institute. He has written books and articles in the field of administrative law and government regulation. A graduate of Stanford University and Oxford University, he graduated *magna cum laude* from Harvard Law School.

Harry L. Carrico is Chief Justice of the Supreme Court of Virginia following service as circuit judge and as trial justice. Chief Justice Carrico created the Commission on the Future of Virginia's Judicial System. He was previously in the private practice of law and served in the U.S. Navy. Co-Chairman of the National Judicial Council of State and Federal Courts, he is a member of the Committee on Federal–State Jurisdiction of the Judicial Conference of the United States. Chief Justice Carrico has served as President of the Conference of Chief Justices and as Chairman of the National Center for State Courts. He took his law degree from George Washington University Law School.

Theodore Cooper is Chairman of the Board and Chief Executive Officer of The Upjohn Company. Dr. Cooper previously held the positions of Vice Chairman of the Board and Executive Vice President. A former Dean of the Cornell University Medical College, he was Assistant Secretary for Health of the Department of Health, Education and Welfare. Dr. Cooper is a Director of the Upjohn Company; Metropolitan Life Insurance Company; Harris Bankcorp and Harris Trust and Savings Bank; Borden, Inc.; and Kellogg Company. He is a Trustee of St. Louis University and the University of Chicago. He has received numerous awards and honors, including the Gold Heart Award and the Department of Defense Distinguished Public Service Award.

E. Donald Elliott is a tenured professor of Law at Yale Law School, where he has taught since 1981. He also serves as a consultant to the law firm of Fried, Frank, Harris, Shriver & Jacobson, in New York and Washington. He has wide experience in the fields of environmental law, administrative law, and toxic torts. From July 1989 to August 1991, he served as Assistant Administrator and General Counsel of the Environmental Protection Agency. In that position, he served as chief legal advisor to EPA administrator William Reilly and headed a staff of over 125 lawyers with a docket of 450 cases. Before joining EPA, Professor Elliott served for five years as Special Litigation Counsel, Corporate Environmental Programs, General Electric Co., where he was responsible for the defense of GE's toxic tort cases. Professor Elliott is the author of over 30 articles and has lectured widely both here and abroad.

In July 1990, Professor Elliott was named as one of the top lawyers in the country in the fields of environmental law and toxic torts by the *National Law Journal*. He is a graduate of Yale College (Phi Beta Kappa, *summa cum laude*) and Yale Law School. Before joining the Yale Law School in 1981, Mr. Elliott was in private practice with a law firm in Washington, DC (Leva, Hawes, Symington, Martin & Oppenheimer) and served as a law clerk to U.S. District Judge Gerhard Gesell and U.S. Circuit Judge David Bazelon. Elliott has been a consultant to the Carnegie Commission on Science, Technology, and Government; the Federal Courts Study Committee; and the Administrative Conference of the United States, and has been Vice-Chair of the ABA Administrative Law Section's Committee on Separation of Powers.

Kenneth R. Feinberg is in the private practice of law in Washington, DC. Mr. Feinberg has served as Administrative Assistant to Senator Edward M. Kennedy and Special Counsel to the United States Senate Committee on the Judiciary. A former Assistant U.S. Attorney for the Southern District of New York, he has served as Adjunct Professor of Law at Georgetown University Law Center, the Graduate School of Political Management, and as Law Clerk to Chief Judge Stanley H. Fuld, New York State Court of Appeals. Mr. Feinberg was appointed Special Settlement Master, *In re: Agent Orange Product Liability Litigation*; Special Settlement Master, *In re: Eagle-Picher Industries, Inc.* (national asbestos personal injury/wrongful death class action); Special Settlement Master, *In re: Joint Eastern and Southern District Asbestos Litigation* (federal and state asbestos personal injury/wrongful death litigation arising out of exposures at the Brooklyn Navy Yard); Special Settlement Master, *County of Suffolk, et al. v. Long Island Lighting Co., et al.* (Shoreham Nuclear Facility class action); Special Settlement Master, *In re: Asbestos Personal Injury Litigation* (asbestos personal injury/wrongful death litigation pending in the Maryland State courts); Special Settlement Master, *In re: DES Cases* (federal and state personal injury/wrongful death DES litigation); Trustee, Dalkon Shield Claimants' Trust; and Member, Presidential Commission on Catastrophic Nuclear Accidents. He is Arbitrator, American Arbitration Association; Member, National Panel, Center for Public Resources; and Vice-Chair, Committee on Alternative Dispute Resolution, American Bar Association. He graduated *cum laude*, from the University of Massachusetts. Mr. Feinberg took his law degree from New York University School of Law, where he served as Articles Editor of the *Law Review*.

Robert W. Kastenmeier is Chairman of the National Commission on Judicial Discipline and Removal and a Distinguished Fellow of the Governance Institute. A Member of Congress for 32 years, he served as chairman of the subcommittee on courts for over 20 years. Mr. Kastenmeier was appointed by Chief Justice Rehnquist to serve as a member of the Federal Courts Study Committee. He was in the private practice of law and served as justice of the peace in Watertown, Wisconsin. Following service in the U.S. Army and the War Department, he took his law degree from the University of Wisconsin.

Donald Kennedy is President emeritus and Bing Professor of Environmental Studies at Stanford University, where he has held a variety of academic positions—Chairman of the Department of Biological Sciences, Chairman of the Program in Human Biology, Vice President and Provost, and President (1980–1992). Dr. Kennedy was appointed to the Benjamin Scott Crocker Professorship in Human Biology and received the Dinkelspiel Award, the University's highest honor for service to undergraduate education. Dr. Kennedy is a member of the National Academy of Sciences, the Institute of Medicine, and the American Philosophical Society; his research interests centered on nervous systems and the control of behavior. He has served on National Academy of Sciences committees on pesticide use and on improving the world's food supply, and is a director of the Health Effects Institute, Clean Sites, Inc., the California Nature Conservancy, and the California Commission on Campaign Financing. He was Senior Consultant to the Office of Science and Technology Policy in the Ford White House, and he served as Commissioner of the Food and Drug Administration during the Carter presidency. Dr. Kennedy was educated at Harvard University, from which he holds three degrees in biology.

Francis E. McGovern is Francis H. Hare Professor of Torts at the University of Alabama School of Law. Professor McGovern was previously Visiting Professor at Massachusetts Institute of Technology, Senior Associate at Harvard, and in the private practice of law. He is Advisor to the Board of Editors for the Manual for Complex Litigation, and a member of the American Bar Association Commission on Mass Torts and the American Law Institute. He is a graduate of Yale University and the University of Virginia School of Law.

Richard A. Merrill is Daniel Caplin Professor of Law at the University of Virginia School of Law and Special Counsel with the firm of Covington & Burling. Professor Merrill was previously in private practice and also served as General Counsel, U.S. Food and Drug Administration. He is a member of the American Law Institute and the Institute of Medicine. He served on the EPA's Biotechnology Science Advisory Committee, and on two Institute of Medicine Committees, looking at nutrition labeling and at FDA's use of advisory committees in product approval. A Rhodes Scholar, he took his undergraduate and law degrees from Columbia University and a masters degree from Oxford University.

Richard A. Meserve is a partner with the Washington, DC, law firm of Covington & Burling. His practice focuses on legal issues that involve substantial technical content, including environmental and toxic tort litigation, nuclear licensing, and the counseling of scientific societies and high-technology companies. He has served on a variety of committees of the National Academies of Sciences and Engineering. He served as Chairman of the Committee to Provide Interim Oversight of the DOE Nuclear Weapons Complex and of the Committee to Assess Technical and Safety Issues at DOE Reactors. He previously served as a member of two committees that examined controls on high-technology exports. Dr. Meserve is now serving as Co-chairman of the National Conference of Lawyers and Scientists, a group sponsored by the American Bar Association and the American Association for the Advancement of Science. He is a Fellow of the American Physical Society and serves on the Society's Panel on Public Affairs. He is a member of the Advisory Council of the Princeton Plasma Physics Laboratory; of the Advisory Board of the MIT Center for Technology, Policy, and Industrial Development; and of the Board of Overseers for the Natural Sciences for Tufts University. He served for four years as legal counsel to the President's Science and Technology Advisor, where he worked on policies relating to the health of science, industrial innovation, and energy. He was also formerly a clerk to Justice Harry A. Blackmun, United States Supreme Court, and to Judge Benjamin Kaplan, Massachusetts Supreme Judicial Court. Dr. Meserve received a B.A. from Tufts University, a Ph.D. in Applied Physics from Stanford University, and a J.D. from Harvard Law School.

Gilbert S. Omenn is Professor of Medicine and of Environmental Health and Dean of the School of Public Health and Community Medicine at the University of Washington, Seattle. He is Principal Investigator of the Carotene and Retinol Efficacy Trial (CARET) to prevent lung cancer and Director of the Center for Health Promotion in Older Adults. Dr. Omenn served as a deputy to Frank Press, President Carter's Science and Technology Advisor and Director of the White House Office of Science and Technology Policy, and then as an Associate Director of the Office of Management and Budget. He served on the National Cancer Advisory Board and the National Heart, Lung and Blood Advisory Council. He was a Visiting Senior Fellow at the Woodrow Wilson School of Public and International Affairs, Princeton University, and then the first Science & Public Policy Fellow at The Brookings Institution, Washington, DC. With economist Lester Lave, he published *Clearing the Air: Reforming the Clean Air Act* (1981). He served on the National Commission on the Environment and now serves on the National Risk Assessment and Risk Management Commission mandated by the 1990 Clean Air Act. He is a member of the Institute of Medicine and served on its Council. He has chaired the Board on Environmental Studies and Toxicology of the National Research Council, and the EPRI EMF Health Effects Technical Advisory Board. He serves on the Board of Directors of Rohm & Haas Company, Amgen, and Immune Response Corporation. He earned his B.A. from Princeton, M.D. from Harvard, and Ph.D. in Genetics from the University of Washington. He was a White House Fellow at the Atomic Energy Commission.

Joseph G. Perpich is Vice President for Grants and Special Programs of the Howard Hughes Medical Institute. Dr. Perpich served as the Associate Director for Planning and Evaluation at the National Institutes of Health and later as Vice President for Planning and Business Development at several biotechnology companies in the Washington area. He joined the Howard Hughes Medical Institute to develop a grants program in science education, which now ranges from grade school activities to postgraduate research training. Dr. Perpich is a graduate of the University of Minnesota Medical School and completed his residency in psychiatry at the Massachusetts General Hospital and the National Institute of Mental Health. He is also a graduate of the Georgetown University Law Center. Dr. Perpich is a fellow of the American Psychiatric Association and a member of the Bar of the District of Columbia. He is a member of the Board of Advisors of the American Board of Internal Medicine. Dr. Perpich has broad experience in science and technology policy—as a congressional fellow with the U.S. Senate Committee on Labor and Public Welfare, Subcommittee on Health, as chairman of the Biotechnology Advisory Committee of the Pharmaceutical Manufacturers Association, as a member of national, state, and local science and technology committees, and on the editorial boards of journals addressing law, science, and society. Dr. Perpich is the author or editor of several articles and books on federal R&D/regulatory policy and the biotechnology industry, including *Biotechnology in Society: Private Initiatives and Public Oversight* (Pergamon Press 1986).

Paul D. Rheingold is with Rheingold & McGowen, P.C. A trial lawyer, Mr. Rheingold represents plaintiffs in mass litigation and product liability. He was previously Lecturer on Law at Harvard Law School and Rutgers Law School, and Adjunct Professor at Fordham Law School. Overseer for the Institute for Civil Justice of Rand Institute, he is Advisor for the American Law Institute Restatement on Products Liability. Mr. Rheingold chairs the Planning Commission for the City of Rye, New York. He is a member of the American Bar Association's Commission on Mass Torts, and previously chaired the Manufacturers' Liability Committee and Special Committee on Punitive Damages of the ABA's Litigation Section. Mr. Rheingold chaired the New York State Bar Association's Committee on Tort Reparations, and was a member of the Advisory Committee on Product Liability for the U.S. Department of Commerce. He is a graduate of Oberlin College and Harvard Law School (*cum laude*).

Maurice Rosenberg is Harold R. Medina Professor of Procedural Jurisprudence Emeritus, Columbia University School of Law. Professor Rosenberg has served as Special Assistant to the Attorney General, and as Assistant Attorney General with the U.S. Department of Justice. He was in the private practice of law following service as Law Clerk to Judge Stanley H. Fuld, New York Court of Appeals. In World War II, he served in the infantry and military government. He has written *The Pretrial Conference and Effective Justice*, 1964; *Conflict of Laws* (with Reese and Hay), 1990; *Civil Procedure* (with Smit and Dreyfuss), 1990; *Justice on Appeal* (with Carrington and Meador), 1976; *Appellate Justice in New York* (with Hopkins and MacCrate), 1983. Professor Rosenberg is a member of the American Academy of Arts and Sciences. He was chairman of the Advisory Council for Appellate Justice, 1971–1976; chairman of the Council on the Role of Courts, 1978–1979; and president of AALS, 1973; and he has been a trustee of the Practicing Law Institute since 1975. Professor Rosenberg is currently serving as academic consultant to the Appellate Judges Seminar Series and as chairman of the ABA Standing Committee on Federal Judicial Improvements. He is a graduate of Syracuse University and Columbia University School of Law, where he was Editor-in-Chief of the *Columbia Law Review*.

Oscar M. Ruebhausen, retired presiding partner of Debevoise & Plimpton, practiced law for nearly 50 years. During those years he engaged in numerous science-related activities. He was General Counsel to the Office of Scientific Research and Development in Washington, DC, from 1944 to 1946. Subsequently, he has chaired, or been a member of, a wide range of commissions, task forces, panels, and committees focused on science/social policy issues. These have been public (at both the federal and state level) and private (supported by foundations or bar associations) in sponsorship. He has also been chairman, or a director, of a number of business corporations and not-for-profit organizations, has written for professional journals, and is a past president of The Association of the Bar of the City of New York. He is a graduate of Dartmouth College (*summa cum laude*) and Yale Law School (*cum laude*), where he was Note Editor of the *Yale Law Journal*.

Pamela Ann Rymer was appointed United States Circuit Judge for the Court of Appeals for the Ninth Circuit (Alaska, Arizona, California, Guam, Hawaii, Idaho, Montana, Nevada, N. Mariana Islands, Oregon, and Washington) following service as United States District Judge for the Central District of California. Judge Rymer was previously in the private practice of law. Judge Rymer is a trustee of Stanford University and was chair of the California Postsecondary Education Commission. She is on the Board of Directors of the Constitutional Rights Foundation and is a member of the Judicial Conference of the United States Committee on Criminal Law and Probation, and the Education Commission of the States, Task Force on State Policy and Independent Higher Education. She is a member of the American Bar Association Civil Justice Reform Coordinating Committee, the State Bar of California Antitrust and Trade Regulation Committee, and the Los Angeles County Bar Association Committee on Professionalism. A graduate of Vassar College, Judge Rymer took her law degree at Stanford University Law School.

Irving S. Shapiro joined the law firm of Skadden, Arps, Slate, Meagher & Flom following his retirement as Chairman of the Board and Chief Executive Officer of the DuPont Company. Mr. Shapiro came to DuPont as an attorney in the Legal Department after serving in the U.S. Department of Justice during the Roosevelt and Truman Administrations, where he specialized in practice before the Supreme Court. His work in the Legal Department emphasized antitrust litigation and providing counsel to various manufacturing departments on a wide range of business problems. During the eight years Mr. Shapiro spent with the Justice Department, from 1943 to 1951, he specialized in practice before the Supreme Court and the various Circuit Courts of Appeal. He worked for eighteen months at the Office of Price Administration in Washington, helping to establish a rationing program at the inception of World War II. He played a major role in the antitrust case of the 1950s and early 1960s that forced DuPont to divest itself of General Motors stock. In 1965 he was appointed assistant general counsel of the company. Mr. Shapiro is a former trustee of the Conference Board and the Ford Foundation. He served for two years as chairman of the Business Roundtable and served two years as vice chairman of the Business Council. He is chairman of the Trustees of the Howard Hughes Medical Institute, and is a member of the American Academy of Arts and Sciences and the American Philosophical Society. He is a Director of AEA Investors Inc. and Morgan Trust Company of Florida. He is a Senior Counselor on the Board of Counselors of Bechtel Group, Inc. He is a Member of the Advisory Council of Wells Fargo & Company. He is a graduate of the University of Minnesota and its law school.

William K. Slate, II, is president of the Justice Research Institute, which is located in Philadelphia and Washington, DC. He previously served as director of the congressionally mandated Federal Courts Study Committee, CEO of the Virginia State Bar, Circuit Executive for the Third Judicial Circuit of the United States, and Clerk of the United States Court of Appeals for the Fourth Circuit; he also served with the United States Department of Justice. He has practiced law, been an adjunct professor of law, judicial administration and management, and was a visiting professor at Seton Hall Law School in Newark, New Jersey. He is the Reporter to the District Court of the Virgin Islands for the Civil Justice Reform Act of 1990. Mr. Slate is an elected member of the American Law Institute and is a member of the ABA Standing Committee on Federal Judicial Improvements. He is a founder of the Council for Court Excellence in Washington DC. Mr. Slate was a member of the Virginia Commission on the Future of the Judiciary Task Force on Technology. A graduate of Wake Forest University and the University of Richmond School of Law, he holds an M.B.A. from the Wharton School of the University of Pennsylvania. He is a graduate Fellow of the Institute for Court Management and an S.M.G. graduate of the John F. Kennedy School of Government at Harvard University. He has also engaged in graduate studies in comparative law at Oxford University.

Patricia M. Wald is United States Circuit Judge for the District of Columbia Circuit. Judge Wald previously served as Chief Judge of the circuit, Assistant Attorney General for Legislative Affairs with the U.S. Department of Justice and Staff Attorney of its Office of Criminal Justice, Litigation Director with the Mental Health Law Project, director of the Office of Policy and Issues with the Sargent Shriver vice presidential campaign, and co-director of the Ford Foundation Drug Abuse Research Project. She also served as an attorney with the Center for Law and Public Policy, the National Commission on the Causes and Prevention of Violence, and the Neighborhood Advisory Committee on Civil Disorder. Judge Wald was a Member of the National Conference on Bail and Criminal Justice and a Consultant for the President's Commission on Law Enforcement and Administration of Criminal Justice. She has been a member of the Committee on Codes of Conduct of the Judicial Conference of the United States and is a member of the Executive Committee of the American Law Institute and its Second Vice President. She is a Fellow with the American Bar Association, a member of the American Academy of Arts and Sciences, and has served with the National

Science Foundation–National Research Council Committee on Law Enforcement and Administration of Justice. She is a graduate of Connecticut College for Women (Phi Beta Kappa, Winthrop Scholar) and Yale Law School (Order of Coif).

Jack B. Weinstein is United States District Judge for the Eastern District of New York. He was Chief Judge from April 30, 1980, to March 31, 1988. Judge Weinstein is a member of the American Law Institute and the American Academy of Arts and Sciences. He has served as a member of the Subcommittee on Federal Jurisdiction of the Committee on Court Administration of the Judicial Conference of the United States; the Advisory Committee on Rules of Evidence; the Special Advisory Group to the Chief Justice on Problems Relating to Federal Civil Litigation; and the Ad Hoc Advisory Committee on the Administrative Office. He was a member of the Judicial Conference of the United States, 1983–1986. Judge Weinstein was Special Counsel to the New York Joint Legislative Committee on Motor Vehicle Problems; Reporter and Consultant on Practice and Procedure to the New York State Temporary Commission on the Courts; member of the Advisory Committee on Practice and Procedure of the New York State Senate Finance Committee; member of the City of New York Advisory Narcotics Council; and County Attorney of Nassau County, New York. He served as Lieutenant in the United States Navy during World War II. He is a graduate of Brooklyn College and Columbia Law School, where he now teaches part-time.

Staff

Jonathan Bender is a Program Associate with the Carnegie Commission on Science, Technology, and Government where he staffs the Regulatory Subgroup of the Task Force on S&T in Judicial and Regulatory Decision Making. Mr. Bender received a B.A. with distinction in philosophy in 1985 from the University of Pennsylvania. While at the University of Pennsylvania he also completed intensive coursework in the natural sciences, with particular attention to the biological basis of behavior. From 1986 to 1988 he did research in the pharmacology of aging at the Medical College of Pennsylvania, and in molecular immunology at the University of Pennsylvania. In 1990 Mr. Bender received an M.P.A. with a concentration in science and technology policy from Columbia University's School of International and Public Affairs. He is currently a candidate for a J.D. from the Georgetown University Law Center, where next year he will be Executive Editor of the *Georgetown International Environmental Law Review.*

Christina E. Halvorson is a Program Assistant with the Carnegie Commission on Science, Technology, and Government. Her primary responsibilities are to the Task Force on Science and Technology in Judicial and Regulatory Decision Making, the Committee on Science, Technology, and Congress, and the *Science & Technology in Congress* bulletin. She received her B.A. with Honors in 1992 from Stanford University in American Studies, with a concentration in Policies and Institutions and a focus on environmental policy. Her previous employment experience includes positions with the World Wildlife Fund, the Jasper Ridge Biological Preserve, Stanford's Civil Engineering department, the National Marine Fisheries Service, the Seattle Aquarium, and the Pacific Science Center.

Mark Schaefer has been a Senior Staff Associate with the Carnegie Commission since 1989. He also serves as the Director of the Commission's Washington office. Prior to joining the Commission, he directed the Congressional Office of Technology Assessment's study of neurotoxic substances and the threat they pose to public health. From 1977 to 1983 he worked in the Office of Research and Development of the U.S. Environmental Protection Agency. He received his undergraduate degree from the University of Washington in 1977, and his Ph.D. in the Neurosciences from Stanford University in 1987. From late 1989 to early 1990 he was a Guest Scholar at the Brookings Institution. Dr. Schaefer originally joined the Office of Technology Assessment as a Congressional Science Fellow in 1987. He has contributed to and edited several publications on environmental and science policy, and has coauthored a number of technical articles in the neurobiology field.

NOTES AND REFERENCES

1. See, e.g., Bob Davis, "White House Seeks to Curb OMB's Hold on Rules with More Open Review Plan," *Wall Street Journal*, February 5, 1993, p. A12.

2. See, e.g., National Commission on the Environment, *Choosing a Sustainable Future: The Report of the National Commission on the Environment* (Washington, DC: Island Press, 1993).

3. William D. Ruckelshaus, "Risk, Science, and Democracy," *Issues in Science and Technology*, Vol. 1, No. 3 (Spring 1985), 19–38.

4. The influential World Commission on Environment and Development, more commonly known as the Brundtland Commission after its chair, Prime Minister Gro Harlem Brundtland of Norway, defines the concept of "sustainable development" as "development that meets the needs of the present without compromising the ability of future generations to meet their own needs." United Nations World Commission on Environment and Development, *Our Common Future* (New York: Oxford University Press, 1987).

5. For example, National Commission on the Environment, *Choosing a Sustainable Future: The Report of the National Commission on the Environment* (Washington, DC: Island Press, 1993); Lester R. Brown *et al.*, *State of the World: A Worldwatch Institute Report on Progress Toward a Sustainable Society* (New York: W. W. Norton and Company, 1993); General Accounting Office, *Transition Series* (Washington, DC: GAO, December 1992).

6. CSIS Strengthening of America Commission, *The CSIS Strengthening of America Commission: First Report* (Washington, DC: Center for Strategic and International Studies, 1992);

Thomas E. Mann and Norman J. Ornstein, *Renewing Congress: A First Report of the Renewing Congress Project* (Washington, DC: American Enterprise Institute/Brookings Institution, 1992).

7. Carnegie Commission on Science, Technology, and Government, *Science, Technology, and the States in America's Third Century* (September 1992).

8. A profuse literature exists on market failures and regulation. See generally David L. Weimer and Adrian R. Vining, *Policy Analysis: Concepts and Practice* (Englewood Cliffs, NJ: Prentice-Hall, 1989); Lee S. Friedman, *Microeconomic Policy Analysis* (New York: McGraw-Hill, 1984).

9. Executive Office of the President of the United States, *Regulatory Program of the United States Government* (April 1, 1990–March 31, 1991), p. 26.

10. During this period the National Institute of Occupational Safety and Health was established within the Department of Health and Human Services to provide scientific research and analysis to undergird OSHA regulations.

11. National Research Council, *Risk Assessment in the Federal Government: Managing the Process* (Washington, DC: National Academy Press, 1983).

12. Environmental Protection Agency, Office of Human Resources Management, *EPA Workforce Snapshots for Fiscal Year 1992* (internal document) (Washington, DC: EPA, 1992).

13. Congress passed the Comprehensive Environmental Response, Compensation, and Liability Act in 1980, reauthorized the Federal Water Pollution Control Act (Clean Water Act) in 1981, and reauthorized the Federal Insecticide, Fungicide, and Rodenticide Act (FIFRA) in 1983. In 1984, Congress passed the Hazardous and Solid Waste Amendments (HSWA) to the Resource Conservation and Recovery Act (RCRA). Although the 1984 legislation was an amendment to the original act, it amounted to what has been described as one of the most restrictive and detailed environmental laws ever enacted. See Roger C. Dower, "Hazardous Wastes" in Paul R. Portney, ed., *Public Policies for Environmental Protection* (Washington, DC: Resources for the Future, 1990), pp. 165–168.

14. Food and Drug Administration, Public Health Service, U.S. Department of Health and Human Services, *Comprehensive Needs Assessment 1994–1997*, 517-023/48005 (Washington, DC: U.S. Government Printing Office, 1991), pp. 2, 11–14.

15. U.S. Environmental Protection Agency, *Unfinished Business: A Comparative Assessment of Environmental Problems, Overview Report* (Washington, DC: EPA, February 1987).

16. U.S. Senate, Committee on Environment and Public Works, Subcommittee on Toxic Substances, Environmental Oversight, Research and Development, "Hearing on the Administration's Strategy to Reduce Lead Poisoning and Contamination" (Washington, DC: U.S. Government Printing Office, February 21, 1991).

17. Office of Technology Assessment, U.S. Congress, *Neurotoxicity: Identifying and Controlling Poisons of the Nervous System*, OTA-BA-436 (Washington, DC: U.S. Government Printing Office, April 1990), pp. 267–268.

18. William G. Wells, Jr., and Mary Ellen Mogee, "Strengthening the Policy Analysis and Research Role and Capability of the Office of Science and Technology Policy, Executive Office of the President," a background paper prepared for the Carnegie Commission on Science, Technology, and Government (May 1, 1990).

19. Office of Management and Budget, "The Work of the Office of Management and Budget" (Washington, DC, June: 1990).

20. National Academy of Public Administration, *Presidential Management of Rulemaking in Regulatory Agencies* (Washington, DC: NAPA, January 1987).

21. Lynton K. Caldwell, "A Constitutional Law for the Environment: 20 Years with NEPA Indicates the Need," *Environment* 31:10 (December 1989), 6–11, 25–28.

22. The Environmental Quality Improvement Act of 1970 (Public Law 91-224) established the Office of Environmental Quality: "There is established in the Executive Office of the President an office to be known as the Office of Environmental Quality. . . . The Chairman of the Council on Environmental Quality established by Public Law 91-190 shall be the Director of the Office. There shall be in the Office a Deputy Director who shall be appointed by the President, with the advice and consent of the Senate."

23. *Blueprint for the Environment: Advice to the President from America's Environmental Community* (Washington, DC: November 1988).

24. Carnegie Commission on Science, Technology, and Government, *E³: Organizing for Environment, Energy, and the Economy in the Executive Branch of the U.S. Government* (October 1991).

25. A "major rule" is a regulation that will likely result in an annual effect on the economy of $100 million or more, or that will otherwise exert a significant adverse effect on the economy. *See* Executive Order 12291 §3(b).

26. See National Academy of Public Administration, *Presidential Management of Rulemaking in Regulatory Agencies* (Washington, DC: NAPA, January 1987).

27. Bob Woodward and David S. Broder, "Quayle's Group Makes the Rules," *Washington Post*, January 9, 1992, p. A17.

28. "Tunnel vision" describes a phenomenon wherein individual agencies view their statutory goals as the sole elements of the regulatory universe and behave accordingly.

29. See, e.g., Christopher DeMuth and Douglas Ginsberg, "White House Review of Agency Rulemaking," 99 *Harvard Law Review* 1075 (1986).

30. For a balanced discussion of issues raised by cost–benefit analyses as practiced in Executive Office review, see, e.g., Thomas O. McGarity, "Regulatory Analysis and Regulatory Reform," 65 *Texas Law Review* 1243 (1987).

31. Herbert L. Needleman *et al.*, "The Long-Term Effects of Exposure to Low Doses of Lead in Children: An 11-Year Follow-up Report," *New England Journal of Medicine* 322(2) (January 11, 1990), 83–88; and Herbert L. Needleman *et al.*, "Deficits in Psychologic and Classroom Performance of Children with Elevated Dentine Lead Levels," *New England Journal of Medicine* 300(13) (March 29, 1979), 689–695.

32. P.L. 98-201, 97 Stat. 1379 *et seq.* (Federal Insecticide, Fungicide, and Rodenticide Act); 40 *U.S.C.* 700–789 (Toxic Substances Control Act); and Public Law 92-573 (Consumer Product Safety Act).

33. 42 *U.S.C.* 7401 *et seq.* (Clean Air Act).

34. *Chevron U.S.A. Inc. v. Natural Resources Defense Council, Inc.*, et al., 467 U.S. 837 (1984).

35. *Corrosion Proof Fittings* v. *Environmental Protection Agency*, 947 F. 2d 1201 (1991).

36. *American Federation of Labor and Congress of Industrial Organizations (AFL-CIO)* v. *Occupational Safety and Health Administration (OSHA)*, 965 F. 2d 962 (1992).

37. 54 *Federal Register* 2332 (1989); 29 *Code of Federal of Regulations* 1910.1000.

38. "Clean Air Act Amendments of 1970," P.L. 91-604, 84 Stat. 1954–2001, *U.S. Code Congressional and Administrative News*, 91st Congress; "Clean Air Act Amendments of 1990," P.L. 101-549, 104 Stat. 2399-2712, *U.S. Code Congressional and Administrative News*, 101st Congress.

39. William D. Ruckelshaus, "Risk, Science, and Democracy," in Theodore S. Glickman and Michael Gough, eds., *Readings in Risk* (Washington, DC: Resources for the Future, 1990), p. 107.

40. National Academy of Public Administration, *Beyond Distrust: Building Bridges Between Congress and the Executive* (Washington, DC: NAPA, 1992), pp. 98–100.

41. Our discussion of IRLG draws both on statements by Task Force members who were associated with it and on Marc K. Landy, Marc J. Roberts, and Stephen R. Thomas, *The Environmental Protection Agency: Asking the Right Questions* (New York: Oxford University Press, 1990).

42. The creation of the Council was in fact a response by agency administrators to a proposed strengthening of RARG's oversight.

43. National Research Council, *Risk Assessment in the Federal Government: Managing the Process* (Washington, DC: National Academy Press, 1983).

44. An example given in the NRC report of a science policy question is whether benign, but possibly precancerous, tumors in test animals should be given as much weight in a risk assessment as malignant tumors. Science can estimate roughly the frequency with which benign tumors in an "average" population will proceed to malignancy, but cannot reliably predict this number in specific circumstances without experimental data. The decision about how to characterize tumors in a given risk assessment, then, depends partially on the assessor's policy preference for either "false positives" (a false showing of hazard), or "false negatives" (a false showing of safety).

45. Office of Science and Technology Policy, "Chemical Carcinogens; A Review of the Science and Its Associated Principles, February 1985," 50 *Federal Register* 10371–10442 (1985).

46. Chaired by the Director of the Office of Science and Technology Policy, the Federal Co-ordinating Council for Science, Engineering, and Technology is composed of department and agency heads or chief technical officials from agencies and departments involved with scientific and technical issues.

47. OSTP, "Coordinated Framework for Regulation of Biotechnology: Establishment of the Biotechnology Science Coordinating Committee," 50 *Federal Register* 47174 (1985).

48. Joseph G. Perpich, "Biotechnology, International Competition and Regulatory Strategies," in Jean L. Marx, ed., *A Revolution in Biotechnology* (Cambridge, U.K.: Cambridge University Press, 1989).

49. *See* Sidney Shapiro, "Biotechnology and the Design of Regulation," *Ecology Law Quarterly* 17:1 (1990), a paper originally prepared for the Administrative Conference of the United States.

50. For an incisive discussion of the tension between science and science policy, and of governmental efforts to craft structures responsive to this tension, see Sheila Jasanoff, "Contested Boundaries in Policy-Relevant Science," *Social Studies of Science* 17:195 (1987); and Sheila Jasanoff, "The Problem of Rationality in American Health and Safety Regulation," in *Expert Evidence: Interpreting Science in the Law* (London: Routledge, 1989).

51. Sidney Shapiro, "Biotechnology and the Design of Regulation," *Ecology Law Quarterly* 17:1 (1990), a paper originally prepared for the Administrative Conference of the United States.

52. With regard to this problem at EPA, see, e.g., Peter F. Guerrero, General Accounting Office, "Testimony before the Subcommittee on Environment, Energy, and Natural Resources, Committee on Governmental Operations, House of Representatives, July 23, 1992" ("[EPA's pesticide] program is plagued by poor data management. . . . As a result of poor management of this data, EPA personnel have great difficulty locating, assessing, and tracking [data submissions]"), pp. 13–14; General Accounting Office, *Environmental Protection Agency: Protecting Human Health and the Environment through Improved Management*, GAO/RCED-88-101 (Washington, DC: GAO, August 1988) ("EPA's information systems have traditionally suffered from incomplete and untimely data"), p. 188.

53. Carnegie Commission on Science, Technology, and Government, *Environmental Research and Development: Strengthening the Federal Infrastructure* (December 1992).

54. U.S. Environmental Protection Agency, *Unfinished Business: A Comparative Assessment of Environmental Problems* (Washington, DC: EPA, 1987).

55. U.S. Environmental Protection Agency, *Reducing Risks: Setting Priorities and Strategies for Environmental Protection*, SAB-EC-90-021 (Washington, DC: EPA, 1990).

56. U.S. Environmental Protection Agency, *Reducing Risks: Setting Priorities and Strategies for Environmental Protection*, SAB-EC-90-021 (Washington, DC: EPA, 1990).

57. U.S. Environmental Protection Agency, *Reducing Risks: Setting Priorities and Strategies for Environmental Protection*, SAB-EC-90-021 (Washington, DC: EPA, 1990), 14.

58. William K. Reilly, "Why I Propose a National Debate on Risk," *EPA Journal* (March/April 1991) 2.

59. An example of a first-order ranking: "List the relative carcinogenicity of all substances in the data base in senescent males under X exposure conditions."

60. The term "risk inventory" was coined by Charles W. Powers, John A. Moore, and Arthur C. Upton in "Improving the Coherence of Federal Regulation of Risks from Hazardous Substances," a background paper prepared for the Task Force on Science and Technology in Judicial and Regulatory Decision Making, Carnegie Commission on Science, Technology, and Government (March 1991).

61. Charles W. Powers, John A. Moore, and Arthur C. Upton in "Improving the Coherence of Federal Regulation of Risks from Hazardous Substances," a background paper prepared for the Task Force on Science and Technology in Judicial and Regulatory Decision Making, Carnegie Commission on Science, Technology, and Government (March 1991).

62. Charles W. Powers, John A. Moore, and Arthur C. Upton in "Improving the Coherence of Federal Regulation of Risks from Hazardous Substances," a background paper prepared for

the Task Force on Science and Technology in Judicial and Regulatory Decision Making, Carnegie Commission on Science, Technology, and Government (March 1991).

63. [The Human Genome] project is seeking a comprehensive mapping of the human genome by coordinating the work of diverse experts just as the Risk Inventory Entity will attempt to 'map' what is known about environmental risks in a comprehensive manner." Charles W. Powers, John A. Moore, and Arthur C. Upton in "Improving the Coherence of Federal Regulation of Risks from Hazardous Substances," a background paper prepared for the Task Force on Science and Technology in Judicial and Regulatory Decision Making, Carnegie Commission on Science, Technology, and Government (March 1991).

64. To be sure, this diversity has sometimes produced unwarranted confusion within and outside the government, and some harmonization is indicated.

65. We intend in this regard that each agency should construe its mission broadly. The construction should be guided by the agency's enabling legislation, mission statement, and related documents. Thus, substances or problems that are not specifically governed by substantive statutes (e.g., indoor air pollution for EPA) will not escape analysis.

66. A substantial impediment to data sharing between agencies and indeed between offices within agencies is confidential business information (CBI) provisions within certain substantive statutes designed to protect trade secrets. For a discussion of current CBI problems under the Toxic Substances Control Act, see U.S. Congress, Office of Technology Assessment, *Neurotoxicity: Identifying and Controlling Poisons of the Nervous System*, OTA-BA-436 (Washington, DC: U.S. Government Printing Office, April 1990), p. 176.

67. National Research Council, *Interim Report of the Panel to Review Earth Observing System Data and Information System (EOSDIS) Plans* (April 1992).

68. Office of Technology Assessment, U.S. Congress, *Neurotoxicity: Identifying and Controlling Poisons of the Nervous System*, OTA-BA-436 (Washington, DC: U.S. Government Printing Office, April 1990), p. 176.

69. Hampshire Research Associates, *Influence of CBI Requirements on TSCA Implementation*, EPA Contract Number 68-DO-0165/68-DO-0200 (March 1992), p. 35.

70. John D. Graham, Laura C. Green, and Marc J. Roberts, *In Search of Safety: Chemicals and Cancer Risk* (Cambridge, Mass.: Harvard University Press, 1988).

71. In this regard, relative risk analysis would seem to fall somewhere between the traditional categories of risk assessment and risk management, perhaps nearer to risk management.

72. See, e.g., Paul Slovic, "Perception of Risk," *Science* (April 17, 1987) 236:280; Peter Sandman, "Risk Communication: Facing Public Outrage," *EPA Journal* (November 1987), 21.

73. During periods of divided government, regulatory agencies must work especially hard to balance the often conflicting policy guidance received from each branch. We note that the task is not one for the agencies alone. Congress and the President must devise approaches to work cooperatively to develop consistent policies and avoid placing regulatory agencies in a position of choosing between conflicting mandates.

74. These value judgments include administrative considerations like how tractable a given problem is, how much it would cost to control, and how fast controls could be implemented.

75. The leading edge of experimentation with value integration in relative risk analysis currently is state environmental programs. Although state experience was too incomplete at the time of this writing for exploration here, we suggest that interested readers of this report closely watch these experiments with citizen participation in the states, which have been aptly described as our "laboratories of democracy."

76. Bruce L. R. Smith, *The Advisors: Scientists in the Policy Process* (Washington, DC: The Brookings Institution, 1992).

77. David P. Hamilton, "FDA to Form New Science Board," *Science* 257:103 (August 21, 1992).

78. U.S. Environmental Protection Agency, *Safeguarding the Future: Credible Science, Credible Decisions*, EPA/600/9-91/050 (Washington, DC: EPA, 1992).

79. Committee on Post Office and Civil Service, U.S. House of Representatives, *Report and Recommendations of the National Commission on the Public Service* (Washington, DC: U.S. Government Printing Office, 1989).

80. Judge Stephen Breyer, *Breaking the Vicious Circle: Toward Effective Risk Regulation* (Cambridge, Mass: Harvard University Press, in press).

81. Richard N. L. Andrews, "Long-Range Planning in Environmental Health and Safety Regulatory Agencies," a background paper prepared for the Task Force on Science and Technology in Judicial and Regulatory Decision Making, Carnegie Commission on Science, Technology, and Government (May 1991).

82. Science Advisory Board, U.S. Environmental Protection Agency, *Future Risk: Research Strategies for the 1990s*, SAB-EC-88-040 (Washington, DC: EPA, 1988).

83. Food and Drug Administration, Public Health Service, U.S. Department of Health and Human Services, *Comprehensive Needs Assessment 1994–1997*, 517-023/48005 (Washington, DC: U.S. Government Printing Office, 1991).

84. Advisory Committee of the Food and Drug Administration, Public Health Service, U.S. Department of Health and Human Services, *Final Report of the Advisory Committee on the Food and Drug Administration* (Washington, DC: HHS, May 1991).

85. Bernadine Healy, National Institutes of Health, "Testimony before the Subcommittee on Science of the Committee on Science, Space, and Technology, U.S. House of Representatives" (April 7, 1992).

86. Senator William V. Roth, Jr., introduced the Federal Program Performance Standards and Goals Act of 1991 (S. 20) in the 102nd Congress. The bill passed the Senate in October of 1992 but did not pass the House during the 102nd Congress. Senator Roth reintroduced a similar bill, the Government Performance and Results Act of 1993 (again, S. 20), in the 103rd Congress. Representative John Conyers introduced companion legislation (H.R. 826) with the same title in the House.

87. U.S. Environmental Protection Agency, *Environmental Investments: The Cost of a Clean Environment: A Summary*, EPA-230-12-90-084 (Washington, DC: EPA, 1990).

88. Carnegie Commission on Science, Technology, and Government, *Enabling the Future: Linking Science and Technology to Societal Goals* (September 1992).

89. Peter F. Guerrero, "Pesticides: 30 Years Since Silent Spring—Many Long-standing Concerns Remain," statement before the Committee on Government Operations, U.S. House of Representatives, July 23, 1992, GAO/T-RCED-92-77 (Washington, DC: U.S. General Accounting Office, 1992).

90. Peter F. Guerrero, U.S. General Accounting Office, "Pesticides: 30 Years Since Silent Spring—Many Long-standing Concerns Remain," statement before the Committee on Government Operations, U.S. House of Representatives, GAO/T-RCED-92-77 (July 23, 1992).

91. U.S. General Accounting Office, *Toxic Substances: EPA's Chemical Testing Program Has Made Little Progress*, GAO/RCED-90-112 (Washington, DC: GAO, 1990).

92. Richard L. Hembra, U.S. General Accounting Office, "Toxic Substances: EPA's Chemical Testing Program Has Not Resolved Safety Concerns," statement before the Environment, Energy, and Natural Resources Subcommittee, Committee on Government Operations, U.S. House of Representatives, GAO/T-RCED-92-21 (March 18, 1992).

93. U.S. General Accounting Office, *Toxic Substances: EPA's Chemical Testing Program Has Made Little Progress*, GAO/RCED-90-112 (Washington, DC: GAO, 1990).

94. Linda J. Fisher, Assistant Administrator for Prevention, Pesticides, and Toxic Substances, U.S. Environmental Protection Agency, "Testimony before the Subcommittee on Environment, Energy, and Natural Resources, Committee on Government Operations, U.S. House of Representatives" (March 18, 1992).

95. Richard N. L. Andrews, "Long-Range Planning in Environmental, Health, and Safety Regulatory Agencies," a background paper prepared for the Task Force on Science and Technology in Judicial and Regulatory Decision Making, Carnegie Commission on Science, Technology, and Government (May 1991).

96. 5 U.S.C. §§ 551 *et seq.*

97. 5 U.S.C. § 553.

98. 5 U.S.C. § 554.

99. 5 U.S.C. §§ 553(c), 556–557. *See* Stephen Breyer and Richard Stewart, *Administrative Law and Regulatory Policy* (Boston: Little-Brown, 1992), pp. 547–559.

100. 5 U.S.C. § 553. See note 99 above, pp. 559–606.

101. Historically, much of the impetus for this modern practice came from experience with formal rulemaking, which appeared cumbersome, expensive, and time-consuming, in the Food and Drug Administration in the 1960s. See Robert Hamilton, "Rulemaking on a Record by the Food and Drug Administration," 50 *Tex. L. Rev.* 1132 (1972); and "Procedures for the Adoption of Rules of General Applicability: The Need for Procedural Innovation in Administrative Rulemaking," 60 *Calif. L. Rev.* 1276 (1972). That experience, and similar experience of other agencies, led to a recommendation of the Administrative Conference of the United States that Congress should generally avoid requiring formality in rulemaking—Recommendation 72-5, *Recommendations of the Administrative Conference of the United States* (1970–72). The Supreme Court to some extent endorsed the trend from formal to informal rulemaking in *United States* v. *Florida East Coast Ry. Co.*, 410 U.S. 224 (1973). See generally Breyer and Stewart, note 99 above, chapter 6.

102. See Antonin Scalia, "Back to Basics: Making Law Without Rules," *Regulation* 25 (July/August 1981); *NLRB* v. *Bell Aerospace Co.*, 416 U.S. 267, 294 (1974) (NLRB "is not precluded from announcing new principles in an adjudicative proceeding . . . the choice between rulemaking and adjudication lies in the first instance within the Board's discretion").

103. See, e.g., *Mada-luna* v. *Fitzpatrick*, 813 F.2d 1006 (9th Cir. 1987) (INS "Operating Instruction" suggesting factors to be considered in deciding whether to defer individual deportations).

104. Antonin Scalia, "Back to Basics: Making Law Without Rules," *Regulation* 25 (July/August 1981), 26–27.

105. See, e.g., David Shapiro, "The Choice of Rulemaking or Adjudication in the Development of Administrative Policy," 78 *Harv. L. Rev.* 921 (1965); Kenneth Culp Davis, *Discretionary Justice: A Preliminary Inquiry* (Baton Rouge: Louisiana State University Press, 1969) pp. 52–96; J. Skelly Wright, Book Review, 81 *Yale L.J.* 575 (1972); Henry Friendly, *The Federal Administrative Agencies: The Need for Better Definition of Standards* (Cambridge, Mass: Harvard University Press, 1962).

106. 5 U.S.C. § 553(b).

107. 5 U.S.C. § 553(c).

108. 5 U.S.C. § 553(c).

109. See Thomas O. McGarity, "Some Thoughts on 'Deossifying' the Rulemaking Process" background paper prepared for the Carnegie Commission on Science, Technology, and Government (1991); Stephen Breyer, *Breaking the Vicious Circle: Toward Effective Risk Regulation*, ch. 2, section C (Cambridge, Mass.: Harvard University Press, in press); Breyer and Stewart, note 99 above, pp. 606–609.

110. See, e.g., *Motor Vehicle Manufacturers Ass'n.* v. *State Farm Mutual Automobile Ins. Co.*, 463 U.S. 29 (1983) (finding an NHTSA decision "arbitrary and capricious" for lack of articulate analysis and specific comment on "relevant data"). See generally, Breyer and Stewart, note 99 above, pp. 567–592.

111. *Weyerhaeuser Co.* v. *Costle*, 590 F.2d 1011, 1028–31 (D.C. Cir. 1978); see also *Action Alliance of Senior Citizens* v. *Bowen*, 846 F.2d 1449, 1455–56 (D.C. Cir. 1988) (adopting a balancing test as to whether further notice and comment on amendments to initial proposals is required, and finding it not required on the facts); *id.* at 1458–59 (Wald, C. J., dissenting) ("In general, agencies engaged in rulemaking must signal for notice and comment material changes between the proposed rule and the final rule . . .").

112. *United States* v. *Nova Scotia Food Products Corp.*, 568 F.2d 240, 251–52 (2d Cir. 1977).

113. *Id.* at 252 (requiring answers to all "vital questions, raised by comments which are of cogent materiality").

114. See 44 U.S.C. §§ 3503 *et seq.* (establishing the Office of Information and Regulatory Affairs); Executive Order No. 12,291, 3 C.F.R. § 127 (1981) (mandating OMB cost–benefit analysis for major regulations); Executive Order No. 12,498, 3 C.F.R. § 327 (1986) (requiring agencies to submit to OMB an annual "draft regulatory program").

115. Breyer and Stewart, note 99 above, p. 607.

116. 5 U.S.C. § 706(2)(A).

117. Breyer and Stewart, note 99 above, pp. 609–611.

118. 42 U.S.C. § 6901, *et seq.*

119. *See* Thomas O. McGarity, "Some Thoughts on Deossifying the Rulemaking Process," Background paper prepared for the Carnegie Commission on Science, Technology, and Government (1991) pp. 10–13.

120. See, e.g., Richard Pierce, "Two Problems in Administrative Law: Political Polarity on the District of Columbia Circuit and Judicial Deterrents of Agency Rulemaking," 1988 *Duke L. J.* 300.

121. 5 U.S.C. § 553(b)(3). See, e.g., *American Postal Workers Union* v. *United States Postal Service*, 707 F.2d 548 (D.C. Cir. 1983) (changed method of calculation of retirement benefits, reducing the expected benefits of 113,000 workers, without notice and comment, upheld as an interpretive rule under 5 U.S.C. § 553(b)(3)(A)); *Brock* v. *Cathedral Bluffs Shale Oil Co.*, 796 F.2d 533 (D.C. Cir. 1986) (Secretary of Labor's informal "guidelines" on when to cite independent contractors for violating safety standards upheld). But see *Community Nutrition Institute* v. *Young*, 818 F.2d 943 (D.C. Cir. 1987) (unsuccessful attempt by FDA to evade notice and comment requirement by designating "action levels" for aflatoxin as nonbinding policy statements); see generally, Breyer and Stewart, note 99 above, pp. 592–606.

122. This idea is explored further in Stephen Breyer, *Breaking the Vicious Circle: Toward Effective Risk Regulation*, ch. 3 (Cambridge, Mass.: Harvard University Press, in press); Jerry L. Mashaw, *Bureaucratic Justice* 226–227 (1983).

123. Compare, e.g., Contract Work Hours and Safety Standard Act, 40 U.S.C. § 333 (1970) (advisory committee of building trade employee representatives, contractors). See generally, Charles W. Powers, "The Role of NGOs in Improving the Employment of Science and Technology in Environmental Management," Working Paper prepared for the Task Force on Nongovernmental Organizations, Carnegie Commission on Science, Technology, and Government (May 1991); Charles W. Powers, "A History of the Health Effects Institute from the Viewpoint of an Interested Participant/Observer" (unpublished manuscript, November 1991). For discussion of agency practices of consultation with scientific experts, see Sheila Jasanoff, *The Fifth Branch: Science Advisors as Policymakers* (Cambridge, Mass.: Harvard University Press, 1990) chs. 5, 10 (1990).

124. Compare 15 U.S.C. § 57a(c)(4) (allowing the Federal Trade Commission to restrict *cross-examination* similarly in its rulemaking proceedings).

125. Compare *id.*, § 57a(c)(3)(B) (allowing for limitation of oral comments).

126. 28 U.S.C. § 1292(b) provides in relevant part: "When a district judge, in making in a civil action an order not otherwise appealable under this section, shall be of the opinion that such order involves a controlling question of law as to which there is substantial ground for difference of opinion and that an immediate appeal from the order may materially advance the ultimate termination of the litigation, he shall so state in writing in such order. The Court of Appeals . . . may thereupon, in its discretion, permit an appeal to be taken from such order . . .: *Provided, however,* That application for an appeal hereunder shall not stay proceedings in the district court unless the district judge of the Court of Appeals or a judge thereof shall so order."

127. See Breyer and Stewart, note 99 above, pp. 607–610.

128. See, e.g., Administrative Conference of the United States, *Procedures for Negotiating Proposed Regulations*, Recommendation No. 82-4, 1 C.F.R. § 305.82-4 (1992), Recommendation No. 85-5, 1 C.F.R. § 305.85-5 (1992); Administrative Conference, *Negotiated Rulemaking Sourcebook* (1990); Phillip Harter, "Negotiating Regulations: A Cure for the Malaise," 71 *Geo. L. J.* 1 (1982); Karen Fiorino and Christopher Kirtz, "Breaking Down Walls: Negotiated Rulemaking at EPA," 4 *Temp. Envtl. L. & Tech. J.* 29 (1985). For an argument for greater use of negotiation in the Superfund context, see Frederick R. Anderson, "Negotiation and Informal Agency Action: The Case of Superfund," 1985 *Duke L.J.* 261.

     As to how reviewing courts should approach negotiated rulemaking, compare Patricia Wald, "Negotiation of Environmental Disputes: A New Role for the Courts?" 10 *Colum. J. Envtl. L.* 1 (1985), with Phillip Harter, "The Role of the Courts in Regulatory Negotiation—A Response to Judge Wald," 11 *Colum. J. Envtl. L.* 51 (1986).

129. Carnegie Commission on Science, Technology, and Government, *Facing Toward Governments: Nongovernmental Organizations and Scientific and Technical Advice* (January 1993).

130. William D. Carey, in foreword to Charles W. Powers, "The Role of NGOs in Improving the Employment of Science and Technology in Environmental Management," Working Paper pre-

pared for the Task Force on Nongovernmental Organizations, Carnegie Commission on Science, Technology, and Government (May 1991).

131. Carnegie Commission on Science, Technology, and Government, *Facing Toward Governments: Nongovernmental Organizations and Scientific and Technical Advice* (January 1993).

132. Charles W. Powers, "The Role of NGOs in Improving the Employment of Science and Technology in Environmental Management," Working Paper prepared for the Task Force on Nongovernmental Organizations, Carnegie Commission on Science, Technology, and Government (May 1991).

133. Donald Kennedy and Charles Powers have proposed this "hub and spokes" model as a means of addressing regulatory policy issues with strong scientific and technical components.

MEMBERS OF THE CARNEGIE COMMISSION ON SCIENCE, TECHNOLOGY, AND GOVERNMENT

William T. Golden (Co-Chair)
Chairman of the Board
American Museum of Natural History

Joshua Lederberg (Co-Chair)
University Professor
Rockefeller University

David Z. Robinson (Executive Director)
Carnegie Commission on Science,
    Technology, and Government

Richard C. Atkinson
Chancellor
University of California, San Diego

Norman R. Augustine
Chair & Chief Executive Officer
Martin Marietta Corporation

John Brademas
President Emeritus
New York University

Lewis M. Branscomb
Albert Pratt Public Service Professor
Science, Technology, and Public Policy
    Program
John F. Kennedy School of Government
Harvard University

Jimmy Carter
Former President of the United States

William T. Coleman, Jr.
Attorney
O'Melveny & Myers

Sidney D. Drell
Professor and Deputy Director
Stanford Linear Accelerator Center

Daniel J. Evans
Chairman
Daniel J. Evans Associates

General Andrew J. Goodpaster (Ret.)
Chairman
Atlantic Council of The United States

Shirley M. Hufstedler
Attorney
Hufstedler, Kaus & Ettinger

Admiral B. R. Inman (Ret.)

Helene L. Kaplan
Attorney
Skadden, Arps, Slate, Meagher & Flom

Donald Kennedy
Bing Professor of Environmental Science
Institute for International Studies and
President Emeritus
Stanford University

Charles McC. Mathias, Jr.
Attorney
Jones, Day, Reavis & Pogue

William J. Perry*
Chairman & Chief Executive Officer
Technology Strategies & Alliances, Inc.

Robert M. Solow
Institute Professor
Department of Economics
Massachusetts Institute of Technology

H. Guyford Stever
Former Director
National Science Foundation

Sheila E. Widnall
Associate Provost and Abby Mauze
    Rockefeller Professor of Aeronautics
    and Astronautics
Massachusetts Institute of Technology

Jerome B. Wiesner
President Emeritus
Massachusetts Institute of Technology

---

* Through February 1993

MEMBERS OF THE ADVISORY COUNCIL, CARNEGIE COMMISSION ON SCIENCE, TECHNOLOGY, AND GOVERNMENT

Graham T. Allison, Jr.
Douglas Dillon Professor of Government
John F. Kennedy School of Government
Harvard University

William O. Baker
Former Chairman of the Board
AT&T Bell Telephone Laboratories

Harvey Brooks
Professor Emeritus of Technology and
    Public Policy
Harvard University

Harold Brown
Counselor
Center for Strategic and International
    Studies

James M. Cannon
Consultant
The Eisenhower Centennial Foundation

Ashton B. Carter
Director
Center for Science and International
    Affairs
Harvard University

Richard F. Celeste
Former Governor
State of Ohio

Lawton Chiles
Governor
State of Florida

Theodore Cooper*
Chairman & Chief Executive Officer
The Upjohn Company

Douglas M. Costle
Former Administrator
U.S. Environmental Protection Agency

Eugene H. Cota-Robles
Special Assistant to the Director
National Science Foundation

William Drayton
President
Ashoka Innovators for the Public

Thomas Ehrlich
President
Indiana University

Stuart E. Eizenstat
Attorney
Powell, Goldstein, Frazer & Murphy

Gerald R. Ford
Former President of the United States

Ralph E. Gomory
President
Alfred P. Sloan Foundation

The Reverend Theodore M. Hesburgh
President Emeritus
University of Notre Dame

Walter E. Massey
Director
National Science Foundation

Rodney W. Nichols
Chief Executive Officer
New York Academy of Sciences

David Packard
Chairman of the Board
Hewlett-Packard Company

Lewis F. Powell, Jr.†
Associate Justice (Ret.)
Supreme Court of the United States

Charles W. Powers
Managing Senior Partner
Resources for Responsible Management

James B. Reston
Senior Columnist
New York Times

TASK FORCE ON SCIENCE AND TECHNOLOGY IN JUDICIAL AND REGULATORY DECISION MAKING

Francis E. McGovern
Professor of Law
University of Alabama

Richard A. Merrill
Professor of Law
University of Virginia

Richard A. Meserve
Attorney
Covington & Burling

Gilbert S. Omenn
Professor of Medicine and Health
Dean, School of Public Health and
    Community Medicine
University of Washington, Seattle

Joseph G. Perpich
Vice President
Howard Hughes Medical Institute

Paul D. Rheingold
Attorney
Rheingold & McGowen, P.C.

Maurice Rosenberg
Professor of Law
Columbia University

Oscar M. Ruebhausen
Retired Presiding Partner
Debevoise & Plimpton

Pamela Ann Rymer
Judge
United States Court of Appeals
    for the Ninth Circuit

Irving S. Shapiro
Retired Chairman and CEO
Dupont Company

William K. Slate, II
President
The Justice Research Institute

Patricia M. Wald
Judge
United States Court of Appeals
    for the District of Columbia Circuit

Jack B. Weinstein
Judge
United States District Court for the
    Eastern District of New York

Senior Consultant

Margaret A. Berger
Professor of Law
Associate Dean
Brooklyn Law School

Staff

Jonathan Bender
Program Associate
Carnegie Commission on Science,
    Technology, and Government

Christina E. Halvorson
Program Assistant
Carnegie Commission on Science,
    Technology, and Government

Mark Schaefer
Senior Staff Associate
Carnegie Commission on Science,
    Technology, and Government